OUR MORNINGS
MAY NEVER BE

Memoirs of a WAAF Sergeant
. . . and Beyond

BY JOAN MACDONALD

Published by

 GENERAL STORE
PUBLISHING HOUSE

Box 28, 1694B Burnstown, Ontario, Canada K0J 1G0
Telephone (613) 432-7697 or 1-800-465-6072

ISBN 1-894263-73-1
Printed and bound in Canada

Layout and design by Derek McEwen

General Store Publishing House
Burnstown, Ontario, Canada

National Library of Canada Cataloguing in Publication

MacDonald, Joan, 1922-
   Our mornings may never be : memoirs of a WAAF sergeant /
Joan MacDonald.

ISBN 1-894263-73-1

   1. MacDonald, Joan, 1922- 2. Great Britain. Women's
Auxiliary Air Force—Biography. 3. World War, 1939-1945—
Personal narratives, British. 4. Pemphigus—Patients—Canada—
Biography.
I. Title.

RL301.M33 2002   940.54'8141   C2002-903824-3

Dedication

With love to Mac, my special Canadian pilot, who exemplifies
the 76 Squadron motto,

"Resolute."

Contents

Acknowledgements

Thank you to our children, John, Lise, Heather and Keith, for their constant interest and active input. To Dr. Gwen Pilkington, author of *Time Remembered*, a dear friend and an honest critic. To Flight Lieutenant Bill Bateman, DFC, for his helpful suggestions. And to Phil Judkins for allowing me to print his toast to 76 Squadron at the reunion in 2001.

Thank you to Will Davies of Toronto for permission to use his painting for the cover. To the Royal Air Force 76 Squadron Association for permission to use the photograph of the memorial window in the Parish Church of All Saints at Holme on Spalding Moor and to Ken Mason for allowing me to use his story.

A special thank you to Mark Blandford, who first encouraged me to write this book and who has been an imaginative and invaluable editor.

CHAPTER 1

The Declaration of War

I WAS SEVENTEEN and living with my family in Wakefield, Yorkshire, England, when war was declared on September 3, 1939. Prime Minister Neville Chamberlain spoke to us all on the wireless at 11:15 a.m. A nation of silent people listened intently to his every word. The die was cast. We were at war with Germany.

That same day, we heard our first eerie, wailing, air-raid siren. This one turned out to be a false alarm, but it gave us the experience of going down to the cellars of our home, which my father had reinforced with extra-heavy beams and made into an air-raid shelter, already equipped with bedding, food and water. The all clear sounded about an hour later. Our family headed upstairs to have the inevitable cup of tea—the eternal comfort for English people—and to discuss what the war might mean for each of us and to try to make plans for our uncertain future.

We were soon in a new world. Heavy blackout curtains draped our windows so that no light could be seen by attacking aircraft, while tape criss-crossed the windows to help prevent flying glass. Air-raid wardens paced around their territories and if so much as a glint appeared they would scream, "Put out that bloody light!" Our cars, when our meagre petrol ration allowed us to drive them, had covered headlights with a mere slit to allow a thin beam of light through.

Our friends, many of them on embarkation leave, began to appear in the uniforms of the three services. They were home to say goodbye before departing to various theatres of war, as yet unknown.

Gas masks were issued. Food began to disappear from the stores. Many English children never saw a banana until the war was over.

The Home Guard was quickly brought into action: groups of grim and tenacious older men who were determined to do their duty for king and country. They paraded with broomsticks while they had no guns. Woe betide anyone who might attempt to invade their precious island home.

All of us did volunteer work of one kind or another. We knitted sweaters and socks for men in the services, rolled bandages, drove ambulances, dug up our beautiful gardens and planted vegetables. My father, who was an infantry major in World War I, became chairman of the War Emergency Committee for the city of Wakefield. Later, as a food executive officer, he was responsible for food rationing. My mother worked in the office of a company making war supplies, while my grandmother, who did all the cooking for us, quickly devised wonderful recipes from our small amount of rations.

Our meat ration was the equivalent of two lamb chops a week. The amount of butter and sugar allowed was minute. Canned goods were on points. Fish was not rationed, but we had to stand in line to get it and it was not always available. Fish cakes were a staple diet, both at home and in restaurants, always made with a little bit of fish and a lot of potatoes. We were trying to be as self-sufficient as we could with our food because we knew German U-boats were lying in wait for our supply ships.

On May 10, 1940, Germany invaded Holland, Belgium and Luxembourg. Prime Minister Chamberlain resigned and Winston Churchill became prime minister of a coalition government. On May 13, he addressed the House of Commons, saying:

> I have nothing to offer but blood, toil, tears and sweat. We have before us an ordeal of the most grievous kind. We have before us many, many long months of struggle and suffering. You ask, what is our policy? I will say, it is to wage war by sea, land and air with all our might and with all the strength that God can give us: to wage war against a monstrous tyranny never surpassed in the dark, lamentable catalogue of human crime. That is our policy. You ask: What is our aim? I can answer in one word: Victory! Victory at all costs, victory in spite of all terror, victory however long and hard the road may be; for without victory there is no survival.[1]

The British people were deeply united. Our mission was clear and we all wanted to join in the war effort. For my part, I decided I would join the nursing auxiliary of our local hospital. Soon I was called to take an evening course. It was very basic and after a few hours I was issued a blue cotton uniform with the letters "N.A." in red on the

---

[1]Quoted in D. Price and D. Walley, *Never Give In: The Challenging Words of Winston Churchill* (Kansas City, Missouri: Hallmark, 1967), p. 3.

front. A white thing I wore on my head looked like part of a nun's habit.

I worked at the hospital for a few hours every Sunday starting at 0900 hours. Because of the wartime shortage of petrol the buses did not start running until 1100 hours. My father had absolutely no petrol to run me around so I walked the three miles to the hospital.

On my first Sunday I had to report to the men's amputation ward—tough beginnings! I walked nervously across the long, glass-enclosed walkway between the two sections of the hospital, hoping there would be no air raids while I was near all that glass. The ward had twenty patients occupying ten beds on each side in perfectly straight lines, red blankets unwrinkled and tucked in neatly. The floors were highly polished. The patients were all ages, some of them civilian casualties, some service personnel wounded in action.

"The sister in charge is a tartar," I was told by another nursing auxiliary who looked scared to death. I walked down the ward trying to look efficient.

An old man called, "Nurse!"

"Who? Me?" I thought. "Well, there is nobody else nearby."

"I need a bottle, quickly," the old man implored. He looked desperate.

I had noticed some metal bottles in a small room at the entrance to the ward. I ran to get one.

"Nurse," the voice was cold and forbidding. The dreaded sister!

"We do not run on this ward. We walk—slowly."

"I'm sorry, Sister," I mumbled.

I gave the old man his bottle. He rewarded me with a relieved smile. I stood by his bed waiting. He used the bottle, then hid it under his blankets.

"I will take that for you," I said.

"No," he argued stubbornly, "I need to keep it here."

I looked around. There was no one else in the vicinity. At this point I decided not to fight with him about it. Another nurse appeared—this time a real one.

"You are to do backs," she said.

"Backs?"

She pointed to a table with trays of talcum powder and alcohol. I gingerly picked one up and approached the first bed. The young man in it turned on his side. I rubbed his back hesitantly, not sure where the back was supposed to end and whether I was supposed to rub his behind, too. Bravely, I did a half-hearted rub in that area and hoped

I was correct. He did not complain. I continued down the ward, gaining confidence as I went along.

A nurse then called me to hold a patient's leg while she changed a dressing. The wound was infected and the smell was horrible. I managed to keep my composure but my legs felt very wobbly and I was hoping I would not faint. My next job: clip the toenails of a disreputable-looking character. As soon as I had finished he jumped out of bed and galloped around the ward in his very short gown. I looked around for help. Everyone in authority seemed to have gone for lunch or disappeared somewhere. I told him, very sternly, to get back into bed at once. To my everlasting surprise he did what I said!

After a few months, the forbidding sister in charge actually recommended me for further training. She wanted me as a full-time nurse's aid. But I had already made another decision: to join the Women's Auxiliary Air Force.

CHAPTER 2

Joining the WAAF

WORKING IN THE HOSPITAL had been gratifying, but I felt that it was important to get into the action; and to be honest I was attracted by the excitement of service life. We had all realized, after Dunkirk (May 26 to June 3, 1940), that if we did not pull together we would be in deep trouble. The evacuation at Dunkirk had touched all our hearts when a thousand boats, varying in size from a Royal Navy anti-aircraft cruiser to dinghies, were sailed across the Channel by their owners from slips along the south coast or along the reaches of the Thames. At least 250 boats were sunk and many of the yacht owners were killed or wounded; but 338,226 men of the British Expeditionary Force and the French Army reached the shores of Britain to fight again. Winston Churchill stated to Parliament after Dunkirk: "We must be very careful not to assign to this deliverance the attributes of a victory; wars are not won by evacuations."

Churchill was the man who now became the voice of a nation, the voice of defiance, the voice of courage, the voice of truth, as he reported:

Even though large tracts of Europe and many old and famous States have fallen or may fall into the grip of the Gestapo and all the odious apparatus of Nazi rule, we shall not flag or fail. We shall go on to the end. We shall fight in France, we shall fight on the seas and oceans, we shall fight with growing confidence and growing strength in the air; we shall defend our island whatever the cost may be, we shall fight on the beaches, we shall fight on the landing grounds, we shall fight in the fields and in the streets, we shall fight in the hills, we shall never surrender; and if, which I do not for a moment believe, this island or a large part of it were subjugated and starving, then our Empire beyond the seas, armed and guarded by the British Fleet, would carry on the struggle until, in God's good time, the New World, with all its power and might, steps forth to the rescue and liberation of the Old.[2]

Of the three services, my preference was the Women's Auxiliary Air Force. There was a lot of appeal in the WAAF recruiting poster: a girl in an air force blue uniform standing on an airfield gazing up at the sky where Spitfires flew. The WAAF corporal at the recruiting centre was friendly, enthusiastic and informative, and I quickly found myself, on August 12, 1941, at nineteen, signing up for the "duration of emergency." I was told that I would be called up in a few weeks. I felt a great sense of adventure.

I waited at home to receive my call-up papers and remember very clearly the day they finally arrived. I was walking down the stairs in our house at Sandal, near Wakefield, one hand trailing languidly on the shining, polished banister. Only yesterday, it seemed, I used to slide down it with great glee. I sat on the middle step feeling like Christopher Robin: "Halfway down the stairs is the stair where I sit, there isn't any other stair quite like it." I felt lazy and lethargic. It was a hot summer afternoon and the sun was striking the stained glass window over the front door, filling the hallway with a soft, rosy glow. The red petals and green leaves in the stained glass stood out in vibrant colour. At the bottom of the stairs on the right, the sun shone on an ancient hat stand holding a collection of raincoats, umbrellas and caps. Rays of sunlight shimmered on the mirror in the centre of the stand, and a brass-handled walking stick caught the reflected glow.

I patted my little Scots terrier, who had come to join me. She sat with a contented sigh, basking in the warmth and luxury of the soft sunlight. Suddenly, her ears pricked up. The postman clumped up the front walk and pushed a handful of letters through the letter box onto the tiled entryway. Quickly released from my lethargic mood I ran down the stairs, clearing the last two in my anxiety to see what the postman had brought. The red reflections from the door streaked over my hand as I reached for the envelopes. I quickly sorted them. Putting most of them on the tray on the table in the hallway, I looked carefully at one, a plain brown envelope with "O.H.M.S." printed across the top—On His Majesty's Service. I flew up the stairs on wings to throw myself on the bed and read the letter I had been waiting for.

---

[2] Ibid., p. 6.

The orders in my utilitarian envelope were quite clear. I was to report to a WAAF depot in Gloucestershire for basic training the following Monday. A rail warrant was enclosed for my journey.

The next few weeks were a hectic blur. I quickly had to learn a totally new way of life. First was the lack of privacy in living in a large hut with a group of other rookies—dressing, undressing and washing in front of strangers of every conceivable type and occupation. We were marched everywhere and inspected regularly. We stood in line for food and medical examinations. We were constantly numbered, kitted for clothing issue and documented.

We were instructed to walk through a van filled with gas, and in the middle of the van ordered to take off our gas masks. We came out choking and gasping. That, we were told, was a reminder. "Always carry your gas masks."

We learned how to pack. When we first slung our unwieldy kit bags over our shoulders most of us fell over backwards! So we became adept at balancing our loads properly. We polished our buttons to a brilliant shine with the help of a brass stick, the end of which slipped over the buttons and prevented the Brasso from staining our new uniforms. We polished the floor space around our beds and stood at attention for inspection of our equipment by our WAAF officers.

We marched and marched and marched again (square bashing) and as we marched we sang our WAAF song:

We volunteered, we volunteered, we volunteered to join
the Air Force
Ten bob a week, nothing much to eat, great big shoes and
blisters on our feet
We volunteered, we volunteered, we volunteered for King and
Country
If it wasn't for the war we'd be where we were before
We volunteered—WE'RE BARMY!

We also quickly learned a whole new RAF vocabulary. To make a mistake was to *put up a black*, for which we were corrected or *torn off a strip*. If we boasted we were *shooting a line*, which people disliked or *took a dim view of*. False information was known as *duff gen*. To give an unwanted job to someone was to *pass the can*, but if they complained about the job they were told not to *get in a flap*. Toilets and washrooms were known as *ablutions*. Our issue of one knife, one fork and one spoon was called our *irons*, which we carried to each meal. After we had finished eating we stood in line outside and sloshed our *irons* through a trough of hot, flotsam-filled water. There must have been masses of germs, but we all stayed very healthy and developed enormous appetites. When our uniforms were issued we were told to take a size larger than we usually wore because we would put on weight; and we all did.

One of the most embarrassing events was the FFI or Free From Infection parade. Once again, we were lined up, while WAAF orderlies looked carefully between our fingers and parted our hair all over our heads. As soon as their fingers probed in our hair we started to feel itchy and could imagine little bugs jumping around. After all, some people had lice and maybe we sat next to one of them and the bugs jumped over. The ultimate disgrace would have been to be told to stand in the line where people were going to be decontaminated. Fortunately, it never happened to me.

When our training was over we felt much more "with it." The bewildered and sometimes frightened girls who had arrived a few weeks before marched smartly in their passing-out parade feeling very proud, as the RAF band played the "Air Force March."

At this point we received our postings to our new stations.

CHAPTER 3

Cranwell

I WAS DELIGHTED to learn that I was to be posted to Cranwell in Lincolnshire to take a course in teleprinting. When I had joined the WAAF I had asked for signals training, thinking my typing would probably be useful. Learning about sending top-secret messages and raid reports from operational stations sounded exciting, and I felt they would make me a definite part of the war effort.

I was also beginning to feel a great sense of belonging in the WAAF and pride in my service. At first we had not been welcomed with open arms, but this was rapidly changing. A typical group captain I met had been with the regular air force for twenty-six years. He believed strongly that war was not a job for women, thinking they would panic under fire. After the Battle of Britain he declared publicly, "I have cause to thank goodness that this country can produce such a race of women as the WAAF of my station."

While the Luftwaffe mercilessly bombed their stations, the WAAF in the operations rooms went on with their duties. There was no panic among them.

They plotted the incoming raiders, allowing the squadrons to disperse and meet the invaders successfully. Some of the WAAF were killed in action as they manned their posts. By their work they ably assisted the young fighter pilots of whom Winston Churchill said with such pride, "Never in the field of human conflict was so much owed by so many to so few."

To be stationed at Cranwell was an extraordinary living and learning experience. As a permanent peacetime station it had good accommodations. The WAAF were billeted in the old married quarters, blocks of brick row houses built around village greens. The greens were now posted with large signboards warning: "OUT OF BOUNDS TO ALL UNAUTHORISED PERSONNEL."

Life here was very strict. We had to salute practically everything that moved, although I do remember an embarrassed young

9

Canadian pilot officer who, when I was about to give him a snappy salute, mumbled, "For God's sake, don't salute me," as he hastily disappeared around the corner. I also remember a WAAF officer tearing me off a strip because I had not noticed her and did not give the required salute. We had many parades, many rules and regulations, but a great social life. The place was a regular league of nations, with boys training for aircrew from all over the world.

There were Australians, Canadians, New Zealanders, Free French, Poles and Norwegians, as well as our own British boys. We realized, as they finished their courses and went off to operational units, that many of them would not live through the next few months; and it made us all the more anxious to do what we could to help.

Because the air force needed to push as many people as possible through the teleprinter school, we worked on a two-shift basis to take our classes. The teleprinters had keyboards similar to a typewriter keyboard. They were electronic and connected by land lines so messages could be sent quickly and secretly. The keyboard had a metal cover so that one had to learn the correct sequence of letters and numbers without looking at the board; in this way we learned to operate them efficiently.

For our first shift classes we had to be on parade at 0500 hours standing at attention outside our houses ready for the march to the teaching huts. It was dark and the corporals in charge marched carrying red lanterns before and after the parade so that no one would run into us. We were given a quick stop at the cookhouse, where we had mugs of hot tea and slabs of bread and jam; and then we were ready to start our training. We worked the early shift for the first half of our course and then we went onto the late shift. Everyone loved that because when we finished work we could go straight to the station hall and dance to the music of the big bands. Our late shift ended at 2030 hours. At 2025 hours without fail everyone stopped work, including the WAAF instructor, and took out lipsticks, compacts and combs to get ready for the big evening ahead. The only exception was if the unofficial lookout at the door called, "He's coming!" This meant that the fatherly flight sergeant (a regular RAF type whom we all felt was a bit confused by all the WAAF invading his territory) was approaching for an inspection. Then the makeup was rapidly hidden and there was a sudden interest in the teleprinters again.

The nightly dances were a good way to meet people of all nationalities and to hear their stories. I met a Polish Air Force officer who was going to London on leave the next day but was not at all happy about it. He considered leave a waste of time. He was anxious to be posted to an operational unit that would enable him to confront the hated Nazis who had invaded his country. His family was still in occupied Poland.

Many of the Norwegians had exciting stories of how they had escaped from occupied Norway in fishing boats, carrying rice paper maps they could eat if the Germans checked their equipment. Sometimes they ran into violent storms and were forced to return to Norway and try again another day. Many of them looked incredibly young in their "sailor suit" uniforms, and indeed they were; young and eager to meet the enemy and help free their homeland.

I dated one Norwegian pilot who was devastated to find out that his father was a quisling (he had co-operated with the Germans). He was very bitter about it and said that he never wanted to see his father again. It was difficult to find the right words that might help him.

* * *

Our first winter at Cranwell was a freezing experience. When we arrived at our instruction huts in the early morning our first duty was to light the coke stove in the corner of the room. It usually took several tries before it started to blaze and then about another two hours for the hut to become warm. We all sat around in our greatcoats and gloves, shivering and complaining when we were told to take our gloves off to practise on our teleprinters.

When my teleprinter course was over, three or four other WAAF and myself were chosen to stay on as instructors. We were all ecstatic, as Cranwell was one of the most active places to be, and we liked the idea of instructing. The only time I had any trouble was when I had to teach a group of Polish airmen who spoke very little English, but we somehow managed to understand each other.

When I became an instructor I was promoted to corporal and there was a lot of extra administrative work to do, such as seeing that the WAAF respected their curfews. One night I was on duty checking to see that the girls were in their houses. The row houses were all in a line and one checked two bedrooms, walked past an open doorway and then went on to check the two bedrooms in the next house. It was after lights out, and the battery of my torch was growing weaker and weaker as I stumbled along with just a little bit of moonlight shining through the windows. I started to walk into what I thought was a bedroom and instead walked right off the top of the stairs, falling all

Corporal Joan Hemingway at Cranwell   JOAN MACDONALD

the way down to the bottom. I ended up with an enormous black eye. I was relieved to be all in one piece but very annoyed about the black eye because I had a first date with a smashing pilot the next evening. Makeup helped a little but I had to put up with a lot of teasing.

* * *

England was now in a desperate situation. U-boats were causing havoc in the Atlantic, the Luftwaffe was bombing British cities, and the British Army had been defeated in Europe and suffered reverses in the Mediterranean theatre.

On December 7, 1941, Churchill turned on his small wireless to catch the nine o'clock evening news and learned that the Japanese had attacked the Americans. He immediately asked for a call to President Roosevelt and within two or three minutes the president was on the line saying, "It's quite true, they have attacked us at Pearl Harbor. We are all in the same boat now."

Churchill said he tried to adjust his thoughts to the supreme world event that had just occurred. He clearly saw it as a turning point in the war. The British Cabinet met at noon on December 8th and His Majesty's ambassador at Tokyo was instructed to inform the Imperial Japanese government in the name of His Majesty's government in the United Kingdom that a state of war existed between the two countries.

* * *

After I had been stationed at Cranwell for about a year and a half, many of the instructors were posted from there to various units all over the United Kingdom. I was sent to Four Group Headquarters in York for a few months and then received a posting to a bomber base at Holme on Spalding Moor. Bomber Command was Britain's main means to retaliate against Germany and I was eager for my new assignment.

Before reporting to Holme, however, I went home on leave.

* * *

In Wakefield everything looked a little shabbier and everyone looked a little more tired, but the morale of the British people was still high and they never lost their sense of humour. My father told me the story of an "unexploded bomb" near the entrance to Wakefield Park. People were evacuated from nearby homes and the bomb squad was called out. When the "bomb" was examined more closely it was found to be a large granite ball from the top of the gatepost that had somehow been knocked to the ground!

Another false alarm was a report of enemy paratroopers landing in Yorkshire. This turned out to be a barrage balloon that had broken loose from its moorings. The balloons were moored over large cities to help prevent German aircraft from making low-level attacks. An Australian I met who was rather disenchanted with England said, "If the barrage balloons were cut this little island would sink!"

The lives of British civilians were controlled by all kinds of bureaucratic regulations from both old and new government departments. Large posters urged everyone to "Dig for Victory"— "Don't eat bread, eat potatoes instead"; and we were warned that "Loose lips sink ships." The signs with the names of the towns and railway stations were taken down so as to confuse the enemy if they invaded, which was a bit confusing for us if we were trying to find our way in a new area. Strict economy was practised. My mother, for example, took her silk stockings to the local clothing store when they laddered (had a run in them), and they were sent away to be invisibly mended. We had only a few clothing coupons a year and did not want to waste them on stockings. An alternative to wearing stockings was to bronze our legs with suntan lotion and draw a straight line up the back with an eyebrow pencil. (This was in the days before pantyhose and all stockings had seams.)

The campaign to get the children out of the big cities to the anticipated safer areas in the country made for strange bedfellows. Some friends of ours offered to take two children, and two brothers aged six and eight were billeted with them. The boys appeared to have lived on a permanent diet of fish and chips and regarded salads as food fit only for rabbits. The eight-year-old arrived home from school one day with a large, flapping hen he had stolen from a farmer. It was hidden under his jacket. He was most disappointed when he was not congratulated on his achievement and was made to take the chicken back to the farmer. There was a lot of adjusting to be done on both sides!

Civilian food rations were smaller than service rations, which made me feel very guilty, especially as my mother saved special things for me when I came home on leave. We were, however, allowed service ration coupons to take on leave, which helped. There was a bit of black marketing but I never heard of anything major. I believe we sometimes ate horsemeat without knowing it when we ordered steak in a restaurant. The local farmer might hand out a few eggs instead of sending them all to a central depot as required by law. If so, everyone kept the secret.

Meanwhile, the bombing had taken its toll. The cricket field behind our house had an enormous hole in it where a bomb had landed. Two semi-detached houses down the road had one house completely destroyed with all the occupants killed, while the other one was still standing with practically no damage. Blast works in mysterious ways.

Some of my friends were home on leave; others would never be home again. A young fighter pilot killed in the Battle of Britain; an army captain missing, believed killed, in the Middle East. A boy who lived on a nearby farm, recently home on leave, departed to return to his station. The next day his mother woke up at two a.m., saying, "Something has happened to Doug." Her husband tried to comfort her by responding that Doug had told them he would not be flying that night, but she would not be consoled. The next morning the dreaded telegram arrived: "We regret to inform you . . ."

My mother had new photographs in our family gallery. One was of my cousin Derek, who had been training as a dentist at Guy's Hospital in London, and found himself digging shelter trenches and helping in operations on bomb casualties. He joined the Royal Navy and went to sea on HMS *Glasgow*. I later had the same photograph in my rogues' gallery at my new station with Derek looking very handsome in his naval officer's uniform. One of the WAAF noticed it one day and asked if that was my boyfriend. I replied that he was my cousin who lived in Ilford, Essex, which happened to be the area she came from. One day, while on leave, Derek was walking down the street when he was approached by an attractive WAAF who saluted him and, with a mischievous grin, said: "Sir, I hear you are Joan Hemingway's favourite cousin!"

Derek wrote to me, saying, "At least you could have given me fair warning."

More family photographs were of my cousin Gerry, a pilot in the Fleet Air Arm; cousin Philip, training as a pilot; and cousin Maisie, who was called up as an ambulance driver in London. Some time before the war, Maisie had spent a few months with a German family to familiarize the son of the family with spoken English. When she found the son was an ardent Nazi, one of the five provincial leaders of the Hitler Youth, she left and returned to England.

My week's leave flew by. I remember that the one important event every day in our home, and indeed in the large majority of homes in England, was listening to the six o'clock evening news on the wireless. The war news was followed very carefully and no conversation was allowed until the news was over.

All through the war but particularly during the darkest days, Winston Churchill's words echoed around the world as he became the personification of Britain's resistance to tyranny and the free world's opposition to Nazi Germany's brutality. By his sonorous speeches he inspired and united the British people. Civilians, exhausted from nightly bombings, living on skimpy rations and often sleeping in air-raid shelters, listened to him, and he gave them pride in themselves. People of the countries occupied by the Nazis risked their lives to listen to him on forbidden wirelesses and he gave them hope. His declamatory prose inspired millions. Who could not but be encouraged by:

Come then, let us to the task, to the battle, to the toil—
each to our part, each to our station. Fill the armies, rule
the air, pour out the munitions, strangle the U-boats,
sweep the mines, plough the land, build the ships, guard
the streets, succour the wounded, uplift the downcast
and honour the brave. Let us go forward together in all
parts of the Empire, in all parts of the Island. There is
not a week, not a day, not an hour to lose.[3]

* * *

Many years later, on his eightieth birthday, Winston Churchill
replied to all the enthusiastic compliments he was receiving that day
by saying: "It was the nation and the race dwelling all around the
globe that had the lion's heart. I had the luck to be called upon to give
the roar."[4]

---

[3] Ibid., p. 3.
[4] *The Oxford Dictionary of Quotations*, Third Ed. (USA: Oxford University Press,
1980), p. 150.

CHAPTER 4

Holme on Spalding Moor

I ARRIVED AT my new posting at Holme on Spalding Moor on a rainy afternoon in the summer of 1943 with my kit bag, gas mask and orders to report to the teleprinter section, where I was to be the non-commissioned officer in charge, accountable to the signals officer.

I now found myself part of a squadron with an incredible spirit and pride. Young men from the British Isles, Canada, Australia, New Zealand, Rhodesia, Norway and other countries were flying together, fighting together against a great evil. Their targets were rocket sites, railroad marshalling yards, aerodromes, submarine pens, munitions factories, army depots and factories, and workers' homes deep in industrial Germany. Nineteen forty-three was a key period when Bomber Command was on the offensive using the new four-engined bombers, the Halifaxes and the Lancasters, with more sophisticated equipment. In January 1943, Churchill and Roosevelt met at Casablanca to agree on future strategy. In particular the military were instructed: "The primary objective will be the progressive destruction and dislocation of the German military, industrial and economic system, and the undermining of the German people to a point where their capacity for armed resistance is fatally weakened."

Holme on Spalding Moor Base was similar to a small town, with a 1,500-acre site sprawling across the Yorkshire Moors. It was the home and workplace for about three thousand airmen and five hundred airwomen, and was the base for the Royal Air Force's 76 Squadron.

On arrival I checked myself into the guardhouse and was told to pick up my issue bicycle. The bike was an absolute necessity, I found later, for getting around the airfield, over the moors to the WAAF site (everything was as dispersed as possible in case of enemy attack), and down to Holme village or Market Weighton for one's social life. My bicycle was a sturdy, unprepossessing black one, with "301" painted in white numbers on her back fender. She was hard to pedal, had unpredictable brakes, and only one speed—slow—but 301 quickly became a big part of my life.

The following morning I used my newly acquired bicycle to ride from the WAAF site to the main camp to report to the Senior Signals Officer, who told me to report for duty on the day shift the next day. I used my day off to explore. Operations were on, judging by the "No Admission" sign glowing red on the ops room door and the huge bombs I had seen being towed across the runways to be loaded on the Halifax bombers. For security reasons I knew there would be no coming and going and no telephone calls into or out from the base. Visiting the countryside or the nearby villages would have to wait, so I checked out the main camp. I saw Flying Control, emergency ambulances, lorries, the officers' mess, hangars with gaping doors and ground crews working on bombers. I stopped for coffee and a dry eccles cake at a NAAFI (Navy, Army and Air Force Institute) van, looked at the sick bay, cycled past the airmens' mess and the equipment stores, and saw a large building with a sign on the door announcing an evening dance. Everywhere I went there were WAAFs, from leading aircraftwomen to flight officers. They cooked meals, and manned telephones, teleprinters and wireless transmitters. They worked on aircraft as flight mechanics and electricians, packed parachutes, drove all kinds of transport, checked equipment, issued flying kits and food rations, loaded ammunition belts, evaluated aerial photography, decoded secret messages, interrogated crews returning from raids and worked in intelligence.

My first day on the base was a mixture of impressions, learning experiences and feelings of intense pride for being part of a squadron that was taking the war into the heart of Germany, often at great cost to itself. The next day, my first on duty, was totally fascinating. After the usual ride across the moors on 301, I reported to the teleprinter room, where I met some of the girls with whom I would be working. I was required to sign the Official Secrets Act and was informed that the teleprinter room was definitely off-limits to all unauthorized personnel.

Names of pilots were being announced on the tannoy (loud-speaker) system. Ops were on with takeoff in the early evening. I learned that one of my duties was to acknowledge the "Form B" when it came over the teleprinter lines, and then deliver it personally to Flying Control. The Form B contained a good deal of information about the coming raid. The target was coded by the name of a fish— Berlin, for example, was "Whitebait." I read the bomb loads, routes in and out, the target indicators and the call signs of the master bombers. I saw that heavy flak was predicted, read the meteorological forecast and the number of aircraft from Four Group taking part in the raid. Each squadron belonged to a group, and the group, in turn, reported to its own headquarters. Ours was in York and the group headquarters reported to Bomber Command near High Wycomb in Buckinghamshire where the commander-in-chief was Air Marshal Harris, better known by his aircrews as "Bomber Harris."

Just before I went off duty I heard that the night's operation was scrubbed, probably because of changing weather conditions over the target. I thought of all the crews who had been briefed and were psyched up for the raid. How did they feel now? Were they relieved because at least they could be sure of living through another night; or were they frustrated because they wanted to get another trip out of the way towards their tour of operations? Then if they were lucky enough and skilful enough to complete their tour they would be sent away for a rest, which in many cases would be a stint as an instructor. I wondered about their reactions, and thought that surely tonight there would be tension-relieving parties in the officers' mess and the sergeants' mess.

CHAPTER 5

Takeoff

THE FOLLOWING POEM was written by a 76 Squadron crewmember who was one of three survivors from an experienced crew shot down over Germany. The poem was started at Holme and completed in a prisoner-of-war camp. I believe it captures the emotions of the crews as they departed on their dangerous missions.

SONG OF ILLUSION AT TAKEOFF

We have done with your day, my friends and I
Done with the breath spoilt hours
For the black, brilliant night is cooling the sky
And the black, brilliant night is ours

We are the children of night, my friends and I
Breathing her purer air
Silhouettes that glide in a rigid world
In a world we find more fair

Through the night while you sleep, undreaming we'll fly
Lonely and quiet souled
Watching stars wheel true across the jet sky
Growing wise before we grow old

With the morning, perhaps, my friends and I
Will sing instead to see
Your flowering dawn reclaim the sky
But our mornings may never be

So we're done with today my friends and I
Done with the faded flowers
Now the cool, brilliant night has claimed the sky
And the cool brilliant night is ours.

Aircrew waiting for operations had many worries and pressures: the bitter cold and darkness for many hours in an uncomfortable plane; poor visibility and mistaken weather forecasts; the extreme danger of intense flak; being coned by searchlights and attacked by enemy fighters; the possibility of having to make an early return because of faulty equipment; the chance of being hit by bombs from one of our own aircraft. A war correspondent who was allowed to go on a mission with one of the crews spoke of the sight of the raging inferno the crews had to face time after time.

What thoughts did the aircrew have as they prepared for their target for tonight? Some of them wrote letters to wives, parents or girlfriends to be mailed only if they failed to return from operations. For any given one hundred aircrew in Bomber Command from 1939 to 1945 the daunting breakdown was:

Killed on operations	51
Killed in crashes in England	9
Seriously injured	3
Prisoner of war	12
Evaded capture	1
Survived unharmed	24

Only the German U-boat crews had a higher casualty rate.

Some of the aircrew carried lucky charms with them on their trips; some of them had premonitions that they would not return from a certain operation. I remember an Australian gunner who told me one evening before takeoff that he was absolutely sure his crew would be in trouble that night. We had a date for dinner in York the following evening and he told me he was taking his regular uniform with him in case they had to land away for some reason and he could change before he kept the date. The next day I heard he was missing in action and later a signal came through from the Red Cross to say that he was a prisoner of war and had broken a leg while parachuting from the damaged aircraft.

Guy Gibson, VC, leader of the famous Dam Busters raid, said one of his frustrations was the impossibility of making non-flyers under-stand the schizoid life of a bomber pilot, who could one day be having a beer in a cozy local pub and the next day be over a target where he was shot at and very often injured or killed. He found it difficult to explain the paradox of English country lanes and German cities and said that people just did not appreciate that after taking off and flying for a couple of hours the aircrews were in the front line of the war night after night and day after day.

They dealt with their losses by saying that certain crews had "bought it," and tried not to look at the empty places in the mess at breakfast.

Group Captain Pelly-Fry, our one-time commanding officer, described things very well: "The more I observed the whole cycle of 76 Squadron activity, from crew briefing right through to takeoff, return and debriefing, the more I realized what a long, tough, uncomfortable and damned dangerous business it was. Worst of all was the fact that each loss—and God knows it happened time and again—was not just one chap in a Spitfire or three in a Boston; this time it was seven young men per bomber."

From my personal experience on the bomber base I also came to know that if there were casualties or aircrew missing in action, if one or two of those Halifaxes out of the maybe twenty-two sent out did not come back, there were no emotional scenes, no tears—except in the privacy of our Nissen huts—because operations had to go on, and probably the next day we would be starting all over again, with the Halifaxes taking off to attack their targets.

Takeoff was always a dramatic time. As we watched the aircraft disappear into the distance, silence settled in. Then we waited for hours on end for their return. How many would never come back? How many whose mornings would never be?

One day I was leaving the WAAF site to go on duty when the sergeant on duty in the guardhouse called me back and told me that no one was allowed to leave the site until further notice. A Halifax had crashed on takeoff with fully loaded bombs that were about to explode. We were ordered to stay as far away as possible. We heard later that all the crew had managed to escape, but there was nothing that could be done about the burning Halifax except to get the other planes dispersed as far away as possible for takeoff. The station commander, who was in the control tower using the tannoy system to order people away from the aerodrome, suddenly found himself in total darkness. The blast had opened a door of a broom closet, sucked him inside, and blown the door shut again! He emerged covered with dust. It was hours before things got back to normal and then there was the large hole in the runway to be fixed.

One evening an excitable Polish pilot refused to take off because he had lost one of his sixteen bombs and was not about to go until the missing bomb was replaced. It was not enough for him to take an incomplete load to the enemy. Our Polish and Norwegian crews had special reasons to want to defeat the Germans, as their countries were still occupied.

When our bomber crews were due to return from their operations, there was a mounting atmosphere of anticipation over our base.

In the kitchen the staff were preparing eggs and bacon (the special operational breakfast). In Flying Control, the R/T operators were waiting to give landing instructions to the pilots. Fire and rescue workers were standing by, and intelligence officers were preparing questions for debriefing.

Teleprinter operators were waiting to send raid reports to Four Group Headquarters, and wireless operators were listening for emergency calls.

Ground crews were waiting for their own particular aircraft to return. (Would it be damaged? What repairs would be necessary? Would it come back at all?) WAAFs in Signals had messages on hand to be sent to next of kin: "We regret to inform you that your son [or husband] is missing on operations." Sick bay was ready for any casualties. WAAF drivers were driving to dispersal points to convey the aircrew back for debriefing. Everyone, from the lofty station commander to the lowest aircraftwoman 2nd class, was waiting—and hoping.

CHAPTER 6

The Ways of the WAAF

ALTHOUGH OUR LIFE in the WAAF at Holme on Spalding Moor Bomber Base was one of intensity and often of fear, living on the edge taught us many things. We learned how important it was to work together and support each other through both triumph and tragedy. We learned to enjoy the lighter side of life both on duty and off. We learned to become friends with a fascinating variety of people of many different backgrounds.

Certainly, our living conditions were primitive. My home was a Nissen hut set amongst some trees at the edge of the WAAF site. The hut had a corrugated metal covering and was shaped like an igloo. It was poorly insulated and the only means of heating was a black, pot-bellied, cast iron stove in the centre that had a voracious appetite for coke and always ate up our supply before the end of the month, when our next small supply was due.

I remember this Nissen hut particularly at two different times of the year. In the freezing, icy winter when the wind swept wildly and ice crackled in the puddles, it was so cold that if we kicked the snow off our shoes it was still unmelted the next morning. In the hot, sultry summer I remember when the only breath of fresh air came through the windows at each end of the hut. One opened inwards for a few inches just over my bed, and once in the middle of the night a cat managed to get through it and jump on me, scaring me half to death!

Our ablutions were across the road from the Nissen hut. Baths with a line painted on them two or three inches from the bottom of the tub to remind us to conserve water; wooden duckboards to walk over concrete floors; rubber bath plugs hidden in a pocket and carefully shared because they had a habit of disappearing and could not be replaced (all rubber was needed for the war effort).

Our Nissen hut held eight WAAF sergeants, all working different shifts, all representing different areas of service. We were in intelligence, motor transport, signals, administration, etc., and were living a life where it was routine for us to watch aircraft flying out on dangerous missions and to hear them returning, often in the early hours of the morning. We would wake up to hear them circling overhead, waiting for their turn to land.

Everything in our Nissen hut was very utilitarian. The blankets were rough, the mattress biscuits were uncomfortable, our issue pyjamas unromantic, our space very limited; but I quickly learned that life could, no matter how grim things got at times, hold a lot of fun and laughter. The WAAF sergeants all cared about each other and they made friendships that in many cases lasted a lifetime.

If one of the sergeants was getting ready to go on a weekend pass to meet her boyfriend, everyone would contribute items of special civilian clothing so that she could look her most glamorous (not to mention the loans of special lipsticks or other rare cosmetics).

One evening, when we were making tea and toast on our black stove, we heard loud bangs on both sides of our Nissen hut. We were sure we were being attacked and were terrified. It was only after some brave soul peeked around the door that we realized with much hilarity that it was just a flock of sheep banging into our abode!

Our sergeants' mess served us hearty but rather unappealing meals. A typical breakfast, for example, might be powdered scrambled eggs, strong tea, and large slabs of white bread and jam. A special Sunday treat for the evening meal was salad and Spam.

Cycling on duty from the WAAF site to the main camp was a routine that kept us healthy, even if our hands froze in the winter in our issue woollen gloves, and our caps failed to prevent the icy blasts from freezing our ears. Riding 301, I skittered across the ruts in the dirt road, splashed through some deep puddles, and passed a group of Nissen huts and some old, rather smelly farm buildings. Finally I came to the road that led through the gate, past the guardhouse to the Signals Section. I left 301 in a rack with other bicycles in various states of disrepair and entered the long, partially underground building that was surrounded by sandbags. In a corridor, under flickering fluorescent lights, I walked past the Map Room, the Intelligence Room and the Operations Room to the Teleprinter Room. Here teleprinters clicked loudly as WAAF operators sent out raid reports; incoming meteorology reports flowed in from a machine in the corner, phones rang, and signals were sent and received.

Life in the Teleprinter Section was either frantically busy, if ops were on, or fairly quiet if no operational flying was underway. On busy shifts we never stopped for a minute, the machines clicking continuously; on quiet shifts we sometimes worked on embroidery or knitting, particularly on the midnight to 0800 shift.

Sometimes signals would come in from the Red Cross indicating that an airman who had been reported missing was now confirmed as a prisoner of war. The condition of runways at various stations was often the reason for a signal. Sometimes there were coded or top priority signals that we had to expedite as "most immediate."

I remember one request for a signal that caused some consternation. A flying officer who had just arrived at Holme on Spalding Moor from another station called and asked to send a message to try to find the whereabouts of his laundry, which appeared to be lost.

"LAUNDRY?" I was totally horrified. I said, firmly, "We do not send signals about *laundry* from this station, Sir."

"Well, they did from my last station," huffed the officer.

"I'm sorry, Sir, I can't do that," I replied. "Would you like to speak to the signals officer?"

"Yes, I would," he responded in a very annoyed voice.

I knocked on the door of the junior signals officer and told him the story.

"Would you like the number of the order that says you can't use the teleprinter lines for this sort of material?" I asked. The junior signals officer indicated that he would. I gave him the information and left the room. The requested signal was never sent.

About two weeks after this episode I went to a dance in the station hall and a very pleasant young flying officer asked me for a dance. We went through the usual routine of, "How long have you been at Holme? What section do you work in?" Suddenly, I noticed him looking at me in a rather strange way.

"You said you worked in Signals," he said. "You wouldn't by any chance be in the Teleprinter Section?"

Something about his voice, at that point, sounded rather familiar. "Laundry?" I queried.

"Yes," he answered. "Luckily my laundry finally caught up with me. I didn't have a chance with your signals officer when he started quoting the number of rules and regulations at me. You wouldn't have had anything to do with that, would you?"

We had a good laugh and went to have a cup of tea and a sandwich together to make our peace.

Many years later, my daughter, annoyed about something I had said she should or could not do, told a friend, "My mother was a sergeant in the WAAF and she never got over it!"

CHAPTER 7

Intimate Issue

A FEW MONTHS AFTER I arrived at Holme on Spalding Moor, an announcement was made that a WAAF clothing parade would be held in the equipment section.

The WAAF was very parsimonious about the issue of new clothing. For starters, you had to present the old, totally worn-out item before you could get a new one. What's more, the person in charge of the clothing parades was a WAAF officer with an eagle eye who was inclined to reject anything that was not ragged, so we took a razor blade and fuzzed things up a bit before presentation.

Indeed, clothing parades were quite an event. The usual items for exchange were bras, garter belts, black woollen knickers rather rudely referred to as "blackouts," blue-and-white flannel pyjamas, grey lisle stockings, black laced shoes, blue shirts with separate collars, and black ties. All these items were very practical, made for warmth and durability. One item we had a particular problem with was our garter belts. The hookup for our stockings was made of some kind of synthetic material that replaced the original rubber, which was now in short supply. The new material was inclined to come unhooked, and the worst scenario was if both hookups came undone at the same time on the same stocking. Then, instead of just a wrinkled, grey stocking, we might end up with a stocking around our ankle—and what if that happened on parade? It was a WAAF's nightmare!

Other necessary items issued to us were sanitary napkins. The rumour was that Lord Nuffield had provided all these supplies for the WAAFs. I have no idea whether this was true, but if so, Lord Nuffield might have been rather upset to know that we had found that the pads made excellent floor polishers and were frequently used for that purpose.

On the day this particular clothing parade was scheduled, the WAAF from our department cycled to work with our various pockets stuffed with items for exchange. The parade was scheduled for 1100 hours, so when we arrived in the office we looked for somewhere to stash our items until that time arrived. We decided on a large cupboard at the far end of the room where paper supplies were stored.

The squadron leader in charge of Signals, a very prim and proper man whom we rarely saw, chose this day, of all days, to do a surprise inspection. Marching briskly into the room with a sharp "Good morning!" he proceeded to inspect every square inch. We stood with bated breath as he pulled open the cupboard door—and out fell a bra, the property of one of our larger WAAF!

The squadron leader turned slightly pink. "Sergeant?" he queried with raised eyebrows.

"Sir, it's for Clothing Parade," I responded.

"I believe there should be a more appropriate place for these . . . er . . . items," he stated.

"Yes, Sir," I answered.

In the next instant the squadron leader marched out of the office and we all looked at each other, not sure whether to laugh or to be afraid we might be put on charge for "inappropriate storage." Looking at the clock we realized there was no time to contemplate our fate, as the clothing parade was in five minutes. So, except for a skeleton staff left behind, we all collected our belongings and left. When we returned, we hid our new shirts and underwear in a corner behind a teleprinter where the weather reports from the meteorological department came clicking in all day long.

The squadron leader never came back to check.

The following week, complete with my new blue shirt and two spare collars, I was sent to a permanent air force station at Calne, in the south of England, to take a teleprinter supervisors' course.

One day, I was sitting in one of the Calne classrooms listening to a lecture when a warrant officer marched in and said, "I am looking for Sgt. Hemingway." The instructor pointed at me.

"The commanding officer would like to see you right away, Sergeant," I was told.

I was petrified. Even though I knew positively I had done nothing wrong, still I thought there must be *some reason* to receive such a summons. The whole class looked at me with pity.

The warrant officer and I marched in step across the parade ground. I finally mustered up enough courage to ask, "Do you know why the commanding officer wants to see me?"

"No," was his curt reply. He obviously was a regular air force type who had no patience with a possibly errant WAAF. He marched me into the CO's office, said, "Sgt. Hemingway, Sir," and left the room. I saluted.

The friendly looking man behind the desk stood up and shook my hand.

"Well," I said to myself, "I don't think I am going to be court-martialled."

"I am Wing Commander Smith," said the officer. "I believe you are a friend of my daughter's. She asked me to find you and invite you to our house for tea tomorrow. She is home on a few days' leave."

I hoped my sigh of relief was not audible.

"Thank you, Sir, I would be delighted to come," I responded. His daughter, Billie, was a fellow WAAF sergeant and a very good friend of mine. We shook hands and the warrant officer was called to escort me back to my classroom.

When I walked in everyone looked very curious and very sympathetic. I could not resist having the final word. "It's OK," I remarked. "The commanding officer just wanted to invite me to tea," and I sat down and continued to listen to the lecture.

I worked very hard on my course and came back to Holme proud of my A-plus mark and my superior rating.

* * *

All WAAF sergeants, no matter what their classification, had to do a certain amount of administrative work, which included taking our turns at acting as duty sergeant. On one of these occasions I was told, together with another WAAF duty sergeant, to attend a funeral service for a local dignitary that was being held at the nearby town of Market Weighton. We were given transportation in an RAF lorry and were delivered to where navy, army, air force and home guard were standing.

An officer in charge of each contingent gave the orders. When it came to the turn of the home guard, a tall, skinny man with a large Adam's apple called out, "Fall out the h'officers." Nobody moved. With a very red face he called out again, "Fall out the h'officers."

A voice from the rear said, "Nay, Bill, if the h'officers all fall out, you won't 'ave enough people left to march."

"Oh," said Bill. "Right turn," and we all started marching smartly down the road. Soon I heard a whisper beside me. "Joan, I've got to go to the bathroom." It had been a long time since we left Holme on

Spalding Moor, with no pit stops, and we had a funeral to attend and more marching to do.

"The hotel," I whispered back.

As we passed the hotel, we slid out of the marching parade, flew up the stairs to the hotel ladies' room, out the side door, and across the parking lot, where we caught up with the parade and joined the others. We hoped the only people who would notice us would be the home guard and that they would not say anything. Then we saw a photographer for the local newspaper busy taking pictures. After two or three days when we heard nothing we thought he must not have seen us—or he had been kind.

* * *

Acting as night duty sergeant in the WAAF guardhouse was a regular chore. One night I was checking in the WAAF and one of the girls was five minutes past her curfew hour of 2300 hours. "You're late," I remarked.

"I'm sorry, Sergeant," she responded. "I just didn't notice the time."

"Where were you?" I asked.

She looked me right in the eye and replied, "I was in the 'edge." I told her it would be a good idea if she stayed out of the hedge and kept track of the time in the future or she would be in trouble. She agreed. I tried not to laugh.

Another night a very pretty and very out-of-breath young WAAF ran into the guardhouse looking very worried. "Sergeant," she blurted, "I'm afraid I have hurt someone and I don't know what to do!"

"What happened?" I asked.

"Well, I had a date and we were walking over the moors back from the village and my date got very fresh. I told him to stop but he wouldn't and I finally got scared and kicked him in the groin and then I ran but he was moaning and I thought I had better tell someone in case he is really in trouble."

I told her to sit down and relax and I called the RAF duty sergeant and told him there might be a problem. He sent one of the duty airmen to check the area my WAAF was talking about. The sergeant called us later and said all was well. The duty airman had found the WAAF's date limping home looking very embarrassed and rather ashamed of himself. The sergeant reported that he would, however, live.

CHAPTER 8

Mac

ONE EVENING I WALKED into the large, noisy hall on the base where an all-ranks dance was being held. The orchestra was playing Glen Miller tunes and the place was hopping.

A tall Canadian pilot with twinkling blue eyes came over to me and asked if he could have the next dance after this one. I was intrigued enough to say yes, thinking this was a different approach and wondering if he always lined up his dances beforehand, as on the old-fashioned dance cards my mother had in her keepsake box at home.

The pilot's name was Mac and I thought he had a nice smile. We had the promised dance and he asked me to have a drink with him. There was a large punch bowl on the table, still about half full, but with only one cup left. Mac suggested we make a loving cup of it! We shared the drink in our cup and then had another dance. After that, I had promised to meet a Rhodesian friend who was coming to the dance later when he returned from flying, and Mac disappeared.

I had often wondered why so many Canadians were attached to an RAF squadron, and had been very interested when this Canadian told me about the British Commonwealth Air Training Plan. It was at the onset of World War II that Vincent Massey, the Canadian High Commissioner to the United Kingdom, proposed that Canada might be able to make a decisive contribution to the war effort by training Commonwealth airmen. The advantages were obvious. Canada was not too far away from the U.K., close to the highly industrialized U.S., and away from the intrusion of the German Air Force. There was plenty of land available to build training facilities. The plan was, according to Winston Churchill, "one of the major factors, and possibly the deciding factor, of the war." English and Dominion air forces were trained on substantially the same types of aircraft, using the same training syllabus, and trained in exactly the same systems, including time and experience in each phase. Fully trained Canadian

George the Sixth,

by the Grace of God, of Great Britain, Ireland and the British Dominions beyond the Seas King, Defender of the Faith, Emperor of India, &c.

To Our Trusty and well beloved *Malcolm William MacDonald* Greeting:

We, reposing especial Trust and Confidence in your Loyalty, Courage and good Conduct, do by these Presents Constitute and Appoint you to be an Officer in Our Active Air Force of our Dominion of Canada from the Sixteenth day of April 1943. You are therefore carefully and diligently to discharge your Duty as such in the Rank of Pilot Officer or in such other Rank as We may from time to time hereafter be pleased to promote or appoint you to, of which a notification will be made in the Canada Gazette, or in such other manner as may for the time being be prescribed by Us in Council, and you are in such manner and on such occasions as may be provided by Us to exercise and well discipline, both the inferior Officers, and other ranks serving under you, and use your best endeavours to keep them in good Order and Discipline. And We do hereby Command them to Obey you as their superior Officer, and you to observe and follow such Orders and Directions as from time to time you shall receive from Us, or any your superior Officer, according to the Rules and Discipline of War, in pursuance of the Trust hereby reposed in you.

In Witness Whereof Our Governor General of Our Dominion of Canada hath hereunto set his hand and Seal at Our Government House in the City of Ottawa this Thirtieth day of June in the Year of Our Lord One Thousand Nine Hundred and Forty-three and in the Seventh Year of Our Reign.

By Command of His Excellency The Governor-General.

James Ralston Minister of National Defence for Air

Pilot Officer Malcolm William MacDonald
Royal Canadian Air Force
Special Reserve

32

aircrew could then be used interchangeably in RCAF or RAF operational squadrons.

Canada played a hugely important role in the war and became the world's biggest air training centre. The British Commonwealth Air Training Plan produced 131,533 aircrew.

I didn't see Mac again for several weeks—he had been away on a course. This time I was waiting in the bus line for York to go on leave, and there was Mac in the lineup with an attractive civilian girl standing next to him. I thought, "Oh well, that's probably his wife or his girlfriend," and I was surprised at how disappointed I felt. But he quickly moved out of the lineup and came over to where I was standing to say, "Hello again!"

We sat together on the bus and discovered we were both going on a week's leave—Mac to London and I to my home in Wakefield. On checking the timetables for our trains we discovered we both had two

"Mac" MacDonald training in Canada
MAC MACDONALD

Flight Lieutenant
Malcolm MacDonald,
RCAF 76 Squadron—
pilot of Halifax Y-Yoke
MAC MACDONALD

or three hours to wait, so Mac invited me to lunch at the Station Hotel.

We went to the bar to have a gin and lime. Lunch was chicken cutlets that tasted like sawdust, but I didn't care at all. We enjoyed our conversation and Mac came onto the station platform to see me off on my train. I had a very definite feeling that this was the beginning of something. I wasn't sure what, but I knew I would be looking forward to getting back to the base after my leave to find out!

I thought about this Canadian often during my leave and frequently told myself that I would be much wiser not to develop any relationship with a bomber pilot whose chances of completing an operational tour were so minimal. I had seen too many broken hearts amongst the WAAFs who had lost their boyfriends. Still, when I returned to Holme on Spalding Moor and reported for duty, I was delighted when the phone rang and I heard that voice with the attractive Canadian accent asking, "Would you like to go down to the village for a drink this evening?" And so our dates began, Mac's operational flying began, and our days of fun and joy and our nights of terror became part of our lives.

I was sure Mac had the same thoughts—that it was better for aircrew not to have commitments, that it was better for them not to have to worry about someone waiting for them to return; but no matter how reasonable and sensible those thoughts were they just didn't work. Every time we parted, Mac said, "I'll give you a buzz tomorrow," and the next time he was not scheduled to fly and I was not on duty, we were together. We just went on with our lives and enjoyed what we could, and that was a great deal.

We laughed a lot. Laughter was the best way to deal with the tension. We even laughed about the "operational twitches": the shrugged shoulders, pulse in the cheek or waggling eyebrows that were the signs of young aircrew growing closer to the end of their tours and worrying about their luck running out. We laughed one day when we went to one of the little cafés in the village to have lunch, both, of course, in our uniforms. Mac asked the waitress if she had any eggs. "No, we don't," she replied. "Don't you know there's a war on?"

We laughed when we went to York and stayed in an ancient hotel run by two ancient sisters who looked at us very suspiciously and carefully put me in a room on the third floor and Mac in a room on the first.

We laughed about our close encounter with the law. We had ridden our bicycles down to the village where we had attended a dance in the village hall, dancing to Victor Sylvester played on cracked records. When we left, it was pitch black outside and, as usual, the blackout was strictly enforced. However, we were all supposed to have dim front lights and tail lights on our bicycles. We had no tail lights for the simple reason that no batteries were available anywhere. As we started on our ride home to base we saw a police van parked across the street, with two policemen checking for lights. We tried to sneak around the side of the building, but a voice yelled, "Stop!"

My adventurous Canadian told me to "ride like hell," and we raced to where the road split. We headed up the road leading to the main camp and soon heard voices, doors banging, and the van starting up in the distance. Mac told me to throw my bicycle into the deep ditch by the side of the road, so 301 and her companion bike disappeared within seconds. We were walking down the road arm in arm when the police van roared by. After spotting us they must have decided they had taken the wrong road. They backed up and headed for the road leading to the WAAF site and we retrieved our bikes and went on our way.

CHAPTER 9

Squadron Discipline

WE FOUND THAT living on a bomber base involved a new set of rules. The discipline was changed. There was very little spit and polish but a lot of pride. The aircrews were too busy flying their risky missions to take the time to be on parade, and the ground crew were too busy spending the extraordinary hours necessary to keep their aircraft in good shape, working outside in all kinds of weather.

Each Halifax had a group of seven people who had their own discipline to follow as they took off on their missions, and they had to work together effectively in order to survive. The pilot was the captain—unlike in the Luftwaffe, where the navigator was the captain—and it was the captain's job to make the decisions: if the aircraft was in trouble, to give the bailout order if necessary, to decide whether to land away, or to try to make it home.

Mac's crew were as follows:

Pilot	Flight Lieutenant Malcolm MacDonald
Navigator	Flying Officer Les Way
Bomb aimer	Pilot Officer Gill Baillargeon
Wireless operator	Pilot Officer Jimmie Low
Mid-upper gunner	Flight Sergeant Dake Daikens
Rear Gunner	Pilot Officer Rick Bronson
Flight Engineer	Sergeant Bill Lucas

Canadians all; with the exception of the flight engineer, who was from England, they were all good friends, and could be quite a party-going group when off duty, but were a very disciplined group in the air.

Discipline was extremely important, both from captain to crew and from aircrew to senior officers. The future of humanity was at stake and it was the crews of Bomber Command who carried their

The crew at Holme on Spalding Moor. Left to right: Bill Lucas, Gill Baillargeon, Jimmie Low, Les Way, Mac MacDonald, Rick Bronson, Dake Daikens   *MAC MACDONALD*

message of defiance into the heartland of the enemy, fighting in conditions of desperate danger.

Seventy-six Squadron was indeed in the front line of attack and, as Dr. Noble Frankland, RAF official historian, wrote, "The ultimate immorality would have been to lose the war against Hitler's Germany."

The amazing thing about our commanding officers was that so many of them had truly exceptional qualities. One after another of these ordinary citizens became heroes, and one after another of them became commanding officers who led from the front.

They were a unique brand of men.

Although they were of many different personalities, they had in common the ability to inspire the respect and confidence of their aircrews. They could certainly discipline an errant airman in no uncertain terms, but they also joined in the fun and games in the officer's mess and at the all-ranks affairs, helping everyone to relax when things were extremely difficult (see Appendix B).

CHAPTER 10

Waiting

ONE OF THE WAAF in the Teleprinter Section wrote this quotation from Alice Duer Miller's "The White Cliffs" in my autograph book:

Lovers in peacetime
With fifty years to live,
Have time to tease and quarrel
And question what to give;
But lovers in wartime
Better understand
The fullness of living
With death close at hand.

Takeoff for operations was often early in the evening. As the Halifaxes lumbered down the runway with their heavy loads we could stand at the edge of the airfield and see the Squadron letters MP on their sides, plus the aircraft letter—for example, "S" for Sugar, "Y" for Yoke, "T" for Tare. Other information of interest was the number of operations that particular aircraft had completed. The ground crew, when the aircraft returned to base, would paint on it a small dark bomb for every night operation and a small white bomb for the daylight ones. Some of the aircraft also displayed more imaginative paintings. "V," for example, was known as Vera the Virgin because of her ostentatious nose art. Her pilot, Flight Lieutenant Bateman, however, reported that when he knew her she was no longer a virgin and pretty well worn out!

If you looked carefully at the small bombs painted on the aircraft you could see that some of them were in the shape of ice-cream cones, representing a mission to Italy. Wing Commander Cheshire said that few of the crews took the trips to Italy very seriously because they did not look upon the Italians as either natural fighters or as being very committed to the war. He reported that although there was a great deal of flak going into the target, as soon as the bombs started bursting, the flak disappeared, indicating the Italians were more interested in getting out of the way!

* * *

An interesting story about insignia on aircraft was told by Lt. Colonel Richard T. Headrick of the United States Air Force. Mrs. Eleanor Roosevelt went to visit an air force squadron at a base at West Palm Beach as they were getting ready to leave for action overseas. The American aircraft had the customary beauties painted on their fuselage. Mrs. Roosevelt did not approve and suggested that the girls be obliterated. A compromise was reached when Mrs. Roosevelt suggested that the girls must have some clothes on. The next day they all wore clothes and Eleanor rather reluctantly accepted this. What she did not know, as the squadron headed overseas, was that the clothing of the young ladies was in water-based paint!

* * *

When Mac was flying on operations I would, whenever possible, cycle over to Flying Control for his takeoff. I would watch until the last throbbing engine faded into the distance, and then my routine of waiting would begin.

There were three different ways for me to cope with these periods. The first one was the best, if I happened to be on duty at the time of the operation. Then, when it came time for the aircraft to return, I would go into the W/T section and put on a spare pair of headphones to listen to the voices of the pilots asking permission to land. Sometimes Mac would be one of the first to call, sometimes almost the last; and sometimes he was forced to land away somewhere. This was when the waiting became horrendous.

I would hear the familiar voices of the pilots: "Hello, Sigmoid—S-Sugar, may I pancake?" and my WAAF friend Bobbie Addison's voice from Flying Control answering, "Hello, S-Sugar, this is Sigmoid. Angels 1,500. Out." This meant that the pilot must circle at 1,500 feet and wait his turn to land. (This also could be a dangerous time as sometimes the Luftwaffe followed our aircraft in and attacked them as they approached the airfield.) The voices that came over the R/T were clipped English voices, Australian accents, the broken English of the Norwegian boys. The hand of the wireless operator was moving down the page checking off, "F-Freddie," "Y-Yoke." And so it went, until the night's work was over. The aircraft that were coming home were home, one with trouble had landed away, and there were two blank spaces on the blackboard in Flying Control for "Time of Return."

My second way of waiting was to volunteer to do tea and rum rations for the returning crews, who were cold and exhausted and still had to face debriefing. The hot mugs of tea and the tot of rum were just what they needed. They would straggle in, chatting with one another.

"Met boobed again with their forecast."

"That flak was really something."

"I hope there's nothing on tomorrow, I've got a date with a blonde in the MT Section."

"I saw two parachutes out of a Halibag shot down on my left."

Eventually, Mac would walk in with a tired smile and seeing him would mean I could finally relax until the next time—one or two nights later.

The third way of waiting was the worst one. I was not on duty, and no volunteers were needed for the tea and rum rations. I would wake up in the early hours of the morning and hear the Halifaxes circling, waiting for their turn to land. I would try to count them, but that was impossible. Cycling to work on the day shift I would meet someone coming off duty. "Any missing?" I would ask.

"Yes, two."

"Do you know who?"

"No, but it was a couple of Canadian crews."

Then I would have to wait, my stomach tied in knots, until I reached the teleprinter section to find out whether Mac had made it back or not.

One night, when the brilliant moonlight was reflected in the dark pools of water on the Yorkshire moors, and I was sleeping uneasily in my Nissen hut, Mac landed at about 0200 hrs, went to debriefing and then made his way over to the WAAF site. He walked into the guardhouse where one of my friends and fellow WAAF sergeants was on duty.

"I need to see Joan," he said.

"Mac, I can't wake Joan up at this time," replied my friend, "and anyway she would be in real trouble if anyone saw you with her at this hour."

"I just need to see her for a few minutes," said Mac.

My friend looked at his white face and tired eyes.

"Bad trip?" she asked with understanding.

"Very."

"All right," she said, "I'll tell her."

It was strictly against rules and regulations, but I didn't hesitate. Mac and I walked down the road in the silvery moonlight, the wind rustling through the bushes. I believe that this was the first time we both knew that our lives would be entwined forever. After a horrendous operational trip, Mac realized that he needed to see me because he truly loved me; and the relief of knowing he had returned safely from one more operation led to the same intense feelings for me. At this time terror increased our happiness because we knew it might be so fleeting. Our love was more intense because of its possible brevity.

Young and in love, we went to London together on leave, knowing that this happiness might not come again; knowing that we must live as fully as we could, while we could. We took the train from York, remembering our first date when we had lunch there, and arrived at bomb-damaged Victoria Station. We hired one of the small, square, black London taxis that could turn on a dime to take us to our hotel, and we had a romantic, exciting four days in the city, which was crowded with service personnel from many different countries and in many different uniforms.

We walked through Hyde Park around the Serpentine, had plowman's lunches in ancient pubs full of shining brass, and listened to the violins at Lyon's Corner House as we ate a fancy English afternoon tea. We strolled hand in hand in the moonlight along the Thames Embankment. We went to the theatre to see a hilarious play whose name escapes me, and to the "pictures" to see *Gone With The Wind*. We danced to the music of the big bands and one morning ran into Mac's navigator, who also was on leave in London, and who was surprised to see me in civilian clothes for a pleasant change. We listened for the nightingale singing in Berkeley Square, thinking of one of our favourite songs by that great wartime singer, Vera Lynn. We fed the pigeons in Trafalgar Square.

It was a magical few days, a pause in the tense waiting and worrying of life on the base; and we decided that when we could both get leave together again, we would get married.

On leave in London: Les Way, Joan, and Mac   JOAN MACDONALD

CHAPTER 11

Christmas at Holme

NINETEEN FORTY-FOUR—Christmas at Holme, a mixture of sad and happy times. Happy because we were together with our friends enjoying the special dinner served by the officers to the other ranks. Sad because so many of the boys were far away from home. ("I'm Dreaming of a White Christmas" sung by Bing Crosby was a tearjerker at this time.) The weather was bitterly cold and the moors were bleak and uninviting.

In an effort to cheer us up, the WAAF sergeants planned a party in their mess for Boxing Day. They decorated with fresh holly and handmade paper chains. Someone had even managed to obtain some "window"—the strips of foil that were dropped out of the aircraft to confuse the enemy radar—and this made a wonderful glittery decoration for our small tree in the corner.

Unfortunately, our plans were not to be.

On Christmas Eve a raid was detailed, then postponed because of hard frost and fog. On Christmas Day the crews, Mac included, were briefed several times, but could not take off because of the heavy, pea soup fog. Stand down finally came in the early evening when the boys ate a belated Christmas dinner and an all-ranks dance was held in the RAF sergeant's mess.

At dawn the crews were called, the officers wakened by their batwomen with a cup of tea, and ordered to briefing, where they found that St. Vith, a small Belgian town, was the target. The town was in the centre of the bulge made by the German advance and the plan was to block all roads leading into the town. This daylight operation was in support of British and American ground forces engaged in the Battle of the Bulge, a last desperate attempt by the Germans to turn the tide for themselves.

After briefing there was another frustrating delay, but at last the order to go was given at midday with an instrument takeoff because of the continuous fog. Only two-thirds of the aircraft got away and then the airfield was closed down. The fog spread across the sea and into northern France.

The attack on St. Vith blocked every road. It was not even possible for the enemy to clear a way through the side streets. Two whole German divisions on their way to critical areas had to make a wide detour that delayed them so much that many of them had no time to dig in before the allies counterattacked.

Mac's flight leader, who was leading the attack, had asked him to fly Q-Queen on his port side, and Flying Officer Woolf, another Canadian pilot better known as Woolfy, to fly R-Roger on his starboard side. As the bombers approached the target the weather became almost clear and the predicted flak was very heavy. Woolf's R-Roger received a direct hit. Horrified, Mac saw the aircraft go up

St. Vith was the target on Boxing Day   MAC MACDONALD

on the port side, then drop down and straighten out. Then he saw three parachutes leave the plane as it dived earthwards towards a fiery death.

* * *

When the weary remaining crews of 76 Squadron returned to base they found that their airfield was again fogged in and they were ordered to divert to another station. Mac was probably the last pilot to ask permission to land at Holme; he had trouble with his bomb doors, which refused to close, and he was, therefore, flying at a slower speed. He was diverted to East Fortune in Scotland, as was his friend, Flight Lieutenant Bill Bateman, and here they were in for a big surprise. On landing at East Fortune, which was a Coastal Command Operational Training Unit, they found a superb welcome. They were invited to join a bash in the officers' mess. All the girls were in evening dress and everyone provided the utmost in Scottish hospitality for those bomber crews who had so unexpectedly arrived at their station.

Flight Lieutenant Bill
Bateman, DFC
MAC MACDONALD

Mac called me at Holme to say that he was safely down. I must admit that the background sound of an orchestra and his description of the girls in their evening dresses made me more than a little envious. Not to mention the fact that many of us were missing dates for our own party in the sergeants' mess! But the main thing was the good news that Mac had returned safely. As always, my relief was incredible. Two days later he was back at Holme with his bomb doors fixed, and the next night he was flying ops again.

* * *

Woolf and his crew were reported missing in action, and a few days later Woolf's brother came to Holme on Spalding Moor to see if there was any more information. The commanding officer asked Mac to talk to him and show him a Halifax. Mac had the sad task of explaining that because of what he had seen and how the aircraft was hit, he felt there was very little chance of Woolfy having survived.

Another episode involving next of kin ended more happily. After a raid on Milan, two crews failed to return. Next of kin were informed and the father of one of the missing men arrived at the base a few days later to pick up his son's personal belongings. A few minutes after the father arrived, a Halifax roared overhead and landed. Among those on board was his son. The pilot reported that his oxygen supply had failed and, not wanting to risk the flight back over the Alps, he had landed in Algeria. He brought back a load of tropical fruits that had not been seen in Britain for years!

CHAPTER 12

The Beginning of the End

As Mac and his crew came closer and closer to the end of their operational tour, the tension rose higher and higher. Originally, the number of missions required to complete a tour was thirty; but when the end was finally approaching the system was changed. It was realized that some of the trips were more difficult than others, and to recognize the inequity a point system was introduced with four points for a German target and three for that of an occupied country. This meant that several pilots, including Mac, were now faced with extra operations to complete their tours.

Extra missions to live through. Extra missions to count down.

Life went on.

I went over to watch more takeoffs, leaning on my bicycle, waving, praying that in a few hours Mac would be on his way home again, circling the station, asking permission to land, joking with Bobbie Addison in Flying Control, whom he called "blonde bombshell."

One evening an ENSA concert visited the station and the crews who were on ops that night came in to watch the first part of the performance before leaving to go to briefing. When they got up to leave, the comedian, who was in the middle of his act, looked very annoyed as he saw a group of people walking out on him. However, he suddenly realized what was happening and stopped his act and began to applaud. The cast and the whole audience joined in as the crews left, and I had a lump in my throat and a feeling of great pride as I watched our boys on their way to their dangerous tasks.

Finally, the night came when both Bill and Mac were scheduled to fly on the last operation of their tours. You can be sure I scheduled myself to serve tea and rum rations that night. The target was Worms. The intent was to bomb a factory that produced sprocket wheels for armoured fighting vehicles for the whole of Germany. Mac was to fly Y-Yoke, one of his favourite and frequently flown Halifaxes. But Y-Yoke and its crew got off to a bad start.

When in position for takeoff, Mac discovered that his constant speed unit on the starboard side of the aircraft was not working. A mechanic was hastily called and within a few minutes everything worked all right, but it meant that they would be several minutes late for takeoff. Every other Squadron aircraft had gone. Flying Control gave Mac the green light and told him he could go straight up the main runway.

Flying alone makes an aircraft much more vulnerable to attack by enemy fighters. Mac asked his navigator to give him the speed that would be necessary to catch up with the main stream of bombers. With the assessed speed he was able to catch up with the squadron aircraft without any incidents, and he then dropped back to normal speed. The bombing was successful, the factory wiped out with the loss of ten Halifaxes from Four Group, mostly to night fighters.

Back at Holme on Spalding Moor I waited anxiously for Mac to return. Several of the pilots walked in, asking, "Is Mac down yet?"

"No," I replied, "but it's early yet."

Bill landed safely. More crews came in, stopping by for their tea and rum rations.

Then I saw a familiar smile, heard a familiar voice: "Hi, Joan." I swallowed hard and tried not to cry. He had made it, my beloved Canadian, one of the few who had come through with a combination of luck and skill. There would be life instead of death in our near future.

It was an incredible, exciting, unbelievably breathtaking night. The tour of operations was over. Forty ops were completed.

CHAPTER 13

Spitfires on Fighter Affiliation

GROUP CAPTAIN PELLY-FRY now asked Mac if, while he was screened, he would like to fly Spitfires and Hurricanes on fighter affiliation. Mac was delighted, because he had always wanted to fly a "Spit" and this would be a great way to spend his "rest period." The group captain also asked him if he would like, when his period with the Spits was over, to come back to 76 Squadron as a flight commander. Mac was honoured. Thankfully, the war in Europe ended before this became necessary.

Flying fighter affiliation meant making practice attacks on the bombers so their pilots would become more proficient at taking evasive action, and their gunners more accurate at "shooting" the Spitfire pilots who were "attacking" them.

Mac loved his Spitfire. When I was home on leave he would sweep over our house so low that he almost hit the chimney tops, and wave.

One day I was waiting at the bus stop opposite our house when I heard the familiar Spitfire roar. An old lady who was standing next to me said, "That should not be allowed. That should be reported. I shall talk to his parents."

I knew she must think it was one of our neighbours who was a pilot. I never said a word. When the bus arrived she was still mumbling as she boarded it. I think that was the only time I did not wave back to Mac!

One day Mac saw four land army girls working in a field and decided to show off with a few aerobatics. He swept low over their heads. The trouble was he was going so fast that when he finally turned around to find them they had disappeared. He had done too big a loop and he never saw the land army girls again.

* * *

We managed to get a few days' leave together and went to my home. Mac had met my parents and it was a mutual admiration society right away, so when we told them our good news about deciding to get married, they were very happy for us. They never worried about their daughter planning to take off for a strange country when this war was over; or, if they did, they kept their worries well hidden. So we had a quiet wedding at our local church with just my family present. I had managed to scrounge enough coupons to allow myself to buy a blue linen suit and a perky blue hat with a veil. Planning a wartime wedding was totally different from planning one in peacetime. There was very little talk about our future—that would have seemed like tempting fate—we just lived and loved for the day.

After the ceremony was over we went to Southport on the train for our honeymoon in a weird old hotel with the bathroom miles down the hall—or so it seemed. The place was so spooky that I truly believed it was haunted; and when I told my new husband there were ghosts around, he kindly escorted me down the long, dark corridor to keep them away from me!

* * *

One day, when I was back at Holme on Spalding Moor, Mac and Bill, who had both been posted to Dishforth, a Canadian unit in Yorkshire flying Spitfires, decided to borrow a couple of aircraft and fly back to Holme for a visit. Mac called me and asked me to borrow a bike for him so we could go to the village for lunch. We had a great pub lunch, cycled back to the base, and the two pilots climbed into their Spits.

As Mac took off I noticed something coming from his aircraft. They had just reached the right heights to do some aerobatics when Flying Control called them and told Mac he was losing petrol. Mac asked Bill to check.

Bill replied, "It is petrol and it's streaming out."

Mac decided he would try and make it back to his home base at Dishforth, thinking he could zigzag between other airfields if he needed to come down sooner. Attempting to get back to base probably had something to do with the fact that they did not have the proper authority to be flying the aircraft!

Just as they got back to the home circuit, Mac's aircraft quit—no more petrol! He called Control and informed them he would have to do a dead stick landing. He put his nose down, maintained a steady speed of 140 miles an hour and headed towards the end of the runway with the usual fighter approach. But as he got closer and closer to the end of the runway, he knew he was flying too fast and that he would have to reduce his speed by sideslipping.

He did this, then straightened out and managed to make a safe landing.

The maintenance problem, he discovered later, was underneath the petrol tank.

I thought of the forty ops that Mac had completed with his crew. I thought of the night he was coned by searchlights—in his opinion one of the most terrifying experiences—escaping them by evasive action.

I thought of the time he brought home his Halifax on three engines on partial power with masses of holes under the wings and damaged propellers.

I thought of all this and realized that one mistake in maintenance could have ended the whole thing.

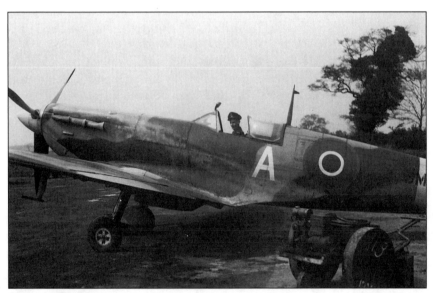

Mac in his Spitfire   MAC MACDONALD

CHAPTER *14*

New Difficulties

And when the dew that lay was gone up, behold,
upon the face of the wilderness there lay a small
round thing, as small as the hoar frost on the
ground. And when the children of Israel saw it, they
said one to another, "It is manna": for they wist not
what it was. And Moses said unto them, "This is the
bread which the Lord hath given you to eat."

Exodus 16: 14-15

AS THE END OF THE WAR came closer, new difficulties and immense problems became more evident in the occupied countries.

Hitler had a carefully planned policy to exterminate the people he subjugated; 6,500,000 Jews and 13,000,000 others were eliminated in his concentration camps, most of them civilians and many of them little children. Ten thousand people died a terrible death in those camps every day, and as the end of war approached this did not stop; the Nazis only worked more feverishly at their horrific programs.

Many people were starving. In April 1945, Queen Wilhelmina was desperately pleading for help from the Allies. The Dutch people were barely existing on a diet of 500 calories a day and were eating nettles and tulip bulbs to stay alive. To make matters worse, the *Reichskommissar*, who was furious because many of these people had worked in various ways in defiance of the Nazi rule, had ordered a total embargo on the movement of food from the agricultural areas to the heavily populated areas of the country.

The way to help the Dutch population was difficult and dangerous, and fell to the air force—in this case to Lancaster squadrons. It was a daunting task for them to deliver food to the starving people, as they had to fly very low, in daylight, over German-occupied territory as easy targets. The plan was called Operation Manna.

General Eisenhower realized that the only way to make food drops successful was to have the co-operation of the Germans; so he told them that the end of their rule was approaching and that any interference with the humanitarian effort to feed the people would be considered a war crime.

Parachutes were in short supply, so other ways had to be found to drop the food. The War Office provided civilian rations and, after much experimenting, the best solution was found to be to pack the food into two burlap sacks that had to be dropped from below 500 feet and at a speed of not over 130 knots. Broadcasts were made to the Dutch people saying where the food drops were to be made.

The first drop was a trial one to establish procedures; 246 Lancasters from One and Three Groups carried a little over 500 tons of food. Eighteen Mosquitoes put down markers for the drop zones. The emotion of the Dutch people was intense. Now they knew they would be able to stay alive. They waved previously hidden flags and tablecloths, made thank-you signs on rooftops and with tulip bulbs. As the planes delivered the food, many Germans shook their fists at them and our bomb aimers happily responded with the "V for Victory" signs! Some of the sacks split open on the runways and the people ran and ate the food right off the ground.

That evening Operation Manna was joined by Operation Chowhound, in which B17Gs of the USAF, 3rd Air Division, dropped packages of ten-in-one rations and K rations. The dropping zones were then extended and the methods of delivery improved with experience. The aircrews willingly dropped their own flight rations of candy, chocolate, etc., tied to a handkerchief or to that day's British newspaper.

By now supplies were beginning to come in by ship and truck and the Lancasters were needed for Exodus, their final big task of the war. They joined other aircraft that had started bringing back prisoners of war, many of them sick and emaciated. At some places the food situation at the camps was so serious that food drops had to be made before the prisoners of war could be liberated.

More than five thousand drops were made by Manna and Chowhound, and only three aircraft were lost: two in a collision and one with an engine fire.

It was a happy occasion for the bomber crews to be dropping food instead of bombs; and the Dutch people have never forgotten them.

CHAPTER 15

"Famously Have You Fought"

BOMBER HARRIS OBSERVED IN 1942, as he watched London burning, that the Germans had sown the wind and would one day reap the whirlwind. This had now happened. The same day the Germans surrendered, May 7, 1945, Four Group was made redundant as a strategic bomber force and most squadrons were transferred to Transport Command.

Winston Churchill had spoken, in his usual inimitable style, of the achievements of the bomber crews:

> The gratitude of every home in our island, in our empire and indeed throughout the world, except in the abodes of the guilty, goes out to the British, Commonwealth and Allied airmen who, undaunted by odds, unwearied in their constant challenge and mortal danger, turned the tide of the world war by their prowess and their devotion.[5]

The war in Europe was now over. Most of the Halifax bombers were flown to Clifton and High Ercall to be sold or, in many cases, to await an unhappy fate in a breaker's yard. It seems incredible that no one, at that time, thought of keeping at least one or two of these famous aircraft; many years later, people were struggling to put one together again.

On May 10, 1945, an Order of the Day was posted on the headquarters notice board at Holme on Spalding Moor. It was written by our commanding officer, Air Chief Marshal Sir Arthur Harris, KCB, OBE, AFC, to the men and women of Bomber Command (see Appendix A). We all felt a sense of great satisfaction

---

[5] From 76 Squadron Association's *Program for the Service of Dedication and Remembrance*, Sept. 4, 1994, p. 1.

when we read this message because of the part we had played, however small, throughout the perilous years of the war. We also felt deep pride as we were reminded in detail of the great variety of Bomber Command's efforts in so many varied directions.

Personally, I felt much empathy as the commanding officer wrote of how his aircrews fought alone, isolated in their crew stations, with menace lurking in each dark minute of the long miles. I knew this to be the simple truth. I also thought the air marshal's final comment, "Famously have you fought, well have you deserved of your country and your allies" was a fitting tribute to the gallant spirit and massive achievements of the aircrews. Their sustained courage and determination prevented all of us from becoming slaves under the swastika.

* * *

In July 1945, when Mac was stationed at No. 1695 BDTF (RCAF), he received a letter from Air Marshal G.O. Johnson, the air officer commanding-in-chief, Overseas Headquarters of the Royal Canadian Air Force in Lincoln's Inn Fields, London.

> Dear MacDonald,
>
> I congratulate you most warmly upon the award of the Distinguished Flying Cross conferred upon you by His Majesty. You must feel a thrill of pride and a satisfying sense of accomplishment since you have brought distinction to yourself and to the Service in this splendid way.
>
> With every good wish for the future.
>
> Yours sincerely,
>
> G.O. Johnson, Air Marshal.

The citation for this Distinguished Flying Cross read:

> For exceptional courage and devotion to duty during numerous sorties against the enemy, he pressed home his attacks with determination and has never let adverse conditions or enemy opposition deter him from completing his allotted tasks.

I felt this was a great tribute to my husband for duty nobly done, and a recognition of his endurance and courage. I was so proud of him!

We were hoping that he would be able to receive this award at Buckingham Palace from King George VI, but time did not allow for this before Mac was sent back to Canada.

Flight Lieutenant Malcolm MacDonald, DFC   JOAN MACDONALD

CHAPTER 16

We Wait Again

THE WAR WITH GERMANY was over and my life with Mac had now become another time of waiting. He was waiting to be demobbed— called back to Canada to start his civilian life and return to his job with the Royal Bank of Canada. I received my discharge from the WAAF and was waiting for a passage on a ship to Canada provided by the Canadian Wives Bureau. As there were many thousands of war brides, we knew it was likely to be a long wait.

And we were both waiting for our new baby to arrive.

Luckily, I was able to stay with my parents. This gave me some special time to spend with them and allowed them to enjoy their new little grandson, John, who arrived two months after Mac was back in Canada.

Months flew by, but there was no call for that voyage to my new land. I even went down to London to the Canadian Wives Bureau to see if there was any way things could be hurried along. I was told there were only two reasons for priority, with so many people waiting. One was if your husband had medical problems and was in hospital, the other if he had bought a farm and needed you to help him run it! Finally, when John was ten months old, I received the long-awaited call for a passage on the *Queen Mary* in July 1946. The night before I left home my feelings were very mixed. Happiness at the prospect of seeing my beloved husband in a few days, sorrow because I would be leaving my family with no idea when I would be seeing them again.

My brother went down to London with me to see me off. The voyage on the *Queen Mary* was a pleasant one. It reminded me of my first days in the WAAF—so many different types of women of every shape, size and personality; so many different attitudes, from joyful anticipation to "If I don't like it, I'm going home." The great ocean liner was still stripped for wartime service. We slept in bunks, with the children in hammock-like cots. The food seemed wonderful to us after the strict wartime rationing; and the weather was perfect. There was one common denominator: We all had children, ranging from babies to pre-schoolers, and we were all facing the big adventure of joining our husbands in a strange land and leaving our families, friends and homeland behind.

The journey took five days.

One morning, when I opened my eyes, I had a strange feeling that something was different. My blue dressing gown, hanging from a hook on the cabin door, was hanging straight down. It had stopped moving from side to side with slow, methodical regularity, as it had been every morning of the voyage. The ship had stopped.

I quickly dangled my legs over my bunk and ran to the porthole to have my first look at Canada, my adopted land, scooping up John from his hammock cot so that he could share this moment with me.

A thick, heavy fog swirling with surly greyness was all I could see.

"So much for all that talk from your daddy about the Sherlock Holmes fogs in England," I said to my little boy. "They have them here, too, and in the summertime!"

We were soon all up on deck. The expressions of the war brides mirrored their curiosity, loneliness, excitement and anticipation as we passed through Customs and Immigration on the ship that early morning. We then disembarked and were loaded onto a shaky old train that had been pulled out of mothballs for the occasion and was sitting in Halifax station ready to take us all to our various destinations right across Canada. Most of us had been waiting to join our husbands for almost a year.

The last time I had seen Mac he had been wearing his pilot's uniform, cap slightly at an angle, Distinguished Flying Cross proudly displayed. He was now working for the Royal Bank in Rock Island, Quebec, and had, he informed me, bought a new suit especially for my arrival.

I wondered how different he would be.

He had rented a "wartime house" built by the government for workers and returning veterans, and had started to build us a cottage on Lake Memphremagog on some land his parents had given us from their farm.

As the train pulled to a stop at Sherbrooke, Quebec, I saw him standing on the platform, with blue eyes twinkling and face lit up with his attractive smile. He had not changed a bit and I was off that train in a minute running down the platform to his waiting arms and handing over his new little son, who had no objection at all to being taken by this handsome stranger.

Our long journey was over. We were on our way home. Our new life was about to begin!

CHAPTER 17

English Spoken Here?

MY NEW ADVENTURES in Canada began with learning a totally new version of the English language. I quickly found there were words with different meanings, expressions that were polite in one country but not in another, strange customs to be learned and mistakes to be made.

My initiation started right away. My luggage was packed into the car trunk (I called it the boot) and maps, my husband explained, were kept in the glove compartment (not in the pigeon hole). I remember fearing that all the traffic was coming right for me, because we were driving on the "wrong" side of the road. We stopped to get some gas (not petrol) and I noticed an attractive lay-by with picnic tables by the side of the road. Mac informed me that was a rest centre. I thought the Canadian language was more practical and not as whimsical as the English.

When we reached our new home, the first thing I wanted to do was call my parents. "Don't call it 'trunks,'" said my husband, "it's 'long distance' over here; and if you need any help ask for information, not inquiries."

My education continued. After allowing me to settle in for a few days a neighbour came to invite me to a baby shower. I had visions of babies sitting in the rain, but she explained it was a party to give gifts to an expectant mother!

I walked to the village store one day and asked for a reel of white cotton. The clerk brought out yards of white material. It was only after much discussion and some expressive hand action that we agreed I needed a spool of white thread.

The numerous errors could be hilarious or at times embarrassing. My first real faux pas was when we were driving out to the country to visit Mac's sister, whom I was about to meet for the first time. My in-laws were with us and I was trying to create a very good impression.

We were delayed and it was getting dark. Knowing this was to be a surprise visit, I said, "Oh dear, I hope we don't have to knock them up."

There was a deathly silence.

Mac explained to me afterwards that to knock someone up in Canada meant to get her pregnant. In England it simply means someone will knock on your door and wake you up. It comes from the days when the mill owners used to hire someone to go around to people's houses with a long stick to knock on their doors and upstairs windows to wake the workers up.

One war bride arrived in Alberta in the middle of the winter absolutely determined to be Canadian and get everything right. At a dinner party she was very surprised, when arriving at her host's home, to find all the women in the bedroom taking off their "panties" along with their coats and boots. With as nonchalant an air as she could manage she also removed her panties, rolled them up and placed them with her hat and coat on the bed. Later, she learned that her Canadian friends were removing their winter woollies worn over their regular panties to help combat the minus twenty-degree weather outside!

When war brides gathered they enjoyed talking about the funny things that had happened to them. Many of us were homesick for a while, but after one trip back to England, most of us realized that we had come to love Canada.

I realized it when flying back to Canada with my young son after a visit with my parents. In Canada I had always listened to the BBC on the radio and thought how good it was to hear the accents of the British announcers. Now the steward on the aircraft was very helpful with my three-year-old and teased him about all the ginger ale he was drinking.

I suddenly thought how good that Canadian accent sounded and I knew that I had made the big transition.

CHAPTER 18

The Four Seasons

FOR SOMEONE WHO had always lived in England there was much to learn about Canada's four seasons.

One very special time of the year was sugaring time, a rite of spring. On a typical March day there was magic in the crisp air. Brilliant sunshine reflected crystal patterns in the deep white snow in the woods. Our senses were inundated with the soft aroma of maple sap boiling in the sugar house, the sweet taste of the golden, sticky syrup as we poured it over pans of snow and wrapped it around forks as it cooled. We watched a pair of tawny horses tossing their heads as they waited impatiently to have a drink of sap from their special buckets, a reward for all their labour. Whether the sugaring was a major production involving miles of piping and thousands of gallons of syrup, or an old-fashioned one using horses to transport the sap from the shining buckets to the sugar house, or even children tapping two or three maple trees in the garden, the wonder of nature was always the same. The old farmers used to say they were born sugaring and it was always the favourite time of the year on the farm when a sugar bush was part of their production.

Sugar bushes are majestic areas. As we crunch through the white snow, dark green evergreens contrast with stately maples while smoke and steam rise from the chimneys of the sugar house to the bright blue sky. Grey squirrels scoot up the tree trunks, blue jays and cardinals flash blue and scarlet. To breathe the cold air feels like taking a drink of clear, icy water from a mountain stream. Children with rosy cheeks play at making angels by lying on their backs and stretching out their arms in the fluffy snow to make wings while gazing at the sky. They eat their fill of syrup poured on snow, enjoy the homemade doughnuts, then eat a huge dill pickle to take away the sweet taste so they can start all over again.

I remember lying in a hospital bed after our daughter was born one March day, watching the sap dripping into the buckets hung on the maple trees just outside the hospital window and thinking what a beautiful day it was.

I remember entertaining friends from England around Christmastime. We collected new, clean snow from our garden, packed it into pans, and boiled up some of our syrup to pour onto the snow and teach them the joys of eating the golden taffy.

Oh, to be in Canada now that April's here?

After maple syrup time, when the piles of snow by the road are dirty and black and the mud on the country roads makes driving difficult, when the city roads are full of potholes and the patches of grass on the lawn are dark brown, then I am homesick for England, with the hazy bluebell woods and the primroses shyly peeping out from the green banks. I think of the wild daffodils growing by the lakeside and the gardens blooming happily around the thatch-roofed cottages.

Luckily, Canada's mud season lasts for only a couple of weeks, and then we are into a brief and beautiful summer.

The most spectacular season of all is the fall—or autumn, as we say in England. People come from all over the world to see the "colours." We call these people "leaf peepers," and they fill our roads with traffic that is most unusual for this area. With the right combination of weather and timing, the fall colours are truly an amazing experience—a glorious vision of deep reds, bright scarlets, brilliant yellows and dark green evergreens that are reflected in the calm waters of the lakes and make a patchwork of blazing colour under the bright blue sky. The gardens are full of richness, and for sheer beauty this season is hard to beat. It does, however, signify the beginning of a long, harsh winter. After the riot of colour there will probably be a heavy rainstorm with strong winds, and that is the end of the fall.

Winter is the time for all the winter sports: skiing—cross-country and downhill—, snowshoeing, curling, skidooing, and skating on the frozen ponds and lakes. Village teams challenge each other to ice hockey games.

On the negative side are the icy roads, the snow to be shovelled out of our driveways and eventually off our roofs, the times when temperatures plummet to forty degrees below zero with the wind chill factor and the only sensible thing to do is to stay in the house, build a blazing fire in the fireplace, and plan next summer's garden from the seed catalogues.

* * *

Mac continued to work on building our cottage and soon we were spending all our summers out at the lake. Our cottage was built on a rock foundation and we had a screened-in porch where we would sit in the evenings and listen to the fish jumping and the haunting cry of the loons. We added a huge fireplace made from stones picked in our field (the rule was that no one, including our three children, was allowed to walk up the hill to the cottage without carrying a stone for the fireplace pile). Eventually we replaced our oil lamps with electricity. Our drinking water we got from a nearby spring.

Mac drove to work every day over dusty country roads, and in the evening the children would listen for the sound of his car rattling over the old covered bridge a mile away so they could have just the right timing for the water skis to be ready when he arrived home.

There are many happy memories of our time at the lake; but one night in particular I will never forget. I woke up around three a.m. to find the whole cottage bathed in silvery moonlight. It was almost ethereal, and I walked onto the porch and saw a broad, shining path reflected on the dark waters below. The trunks of the birch trees around the cottage gleamed luminescent, the water lapped gently on the shoreline, an owl hooted in the distance. I sat on the porch steps thinking back to the moonlit nights at Holme on Spalding Moor, and contemplating how amazing it was that my Canadian pilot had built us this cottage, which was a perfect setting for such a magical night. Then I saw a point of light among the dark trees in the distance, and another, and another: hundreds of fireflies signalling to each other and flashing and darting in an everlasting dance. That memory, like Wordsworth's daffodils, often flashes in my "inward eye that is the bliss of solitude" and I dance with the fireflies.

CHAPTER *19*

Air Force Friendships

SOME OF OUR MOST LASTING and meaningful friendships were made when we were spending our summers at our newly completed cottage on Lake Memphremagog.

In 1947, Ken and Nan Winder, recently returned from England and the war, and more recently returned from visiting Nan's family in Medicine Hat, were wandering around with the intention of visiting the Green and White Mountains, using their tent and camping gear. By what Nan called "unusual and amazing luck," they took a wrong turn and eventually ended up in Fitch Bay in a lovely field. By another chance they saw Mac's dad busy in this field and stopped and asked him, rather timidly, if it would be all right to camp there. Dad MacDonald agreed to their request and informed them that his son and wife lived in the cottage on the hill yonder and would be glad to show them where to get water from the spring, and to help in other ways.

Nan wrote, "We were definitely not experienced campers, nor skilled weather watchers, even my pilot husband. It poured that night in near vengeful torrents. Mac and Joan flew like angels down the hill to retrieve us from our drenched fate and insisted we join them in their cozy cottage. Words could not express our relief and gratitude." Thus began a great friendship. Ken, an RAF Mosquito pilot, and Mac thoroughly enjoyed each other. They fished almost every evening—fly fishing or trolling—while Nan taught me how to paint with oils. Nan and Ken enjoyed our two-year-old, who loved Coca-Cola and would sneak over to their tent, hoping he would be offered one that was cooling in the lake. Our cocker spaniel, Bussie, on the other hand, disgraced himself by stealing a pound of bacon from under the flap of the tent and flying across the field with it, ignoring the screams of Nan and Ken.

The most interesting part for all of us was talking about the years we had just been through. Ken was an Englishman who had been posted to Medicine Hat as a flying instructor with the Commonwealth Air Training Plan and was stationed there for two-and-a-half years. He and Nan married there; and when Ken was posted back to England to fly Mosquitoes on operations, Nan took the risk of making a hazardous trip across the Atlantic to spend the rest of the war years with him. By a strange coincidence her sister, Gwen, who had also married an English pilot who was instructing at Medicine Hat, was given a passage on the same boat. The adventures of a pregnant young Gwen and her sister are well told in Gwen's book, *Time Remembered*, published in 1993. Sadly, Gwen's husband, Tony, was killed on operations shortly after their baby was born. Gwen's book describes the trauma of living in wartime Britain with a new baby, a strange assortment of landladies, and some relatives who were far from welcoming. However, the two sisters stayed together with a varied collection of "waiting wives."

Later on in the war, Harry, Ken's navigator, fell in love with Gwen and her precious little baby, and when the war was over they were married. Both couples decided to live in Canada, and through our meeting with Nan and Ken we became great friends with Gwen and Harry also. Recently, reading a book entitled *Aircrew Memories* containing a chapter by Harry, a flood of memories came back of our many conversations as we all sat on the porch of our cottage watching the sun set and enjoying air force talk.

Ken and Harry flew eighty-three operations together as pilot and navigator on Mosquitoes. They were mostly night intruder and anti-movement patrols (trains, troop convoys etc.), and daylight trips to special targets such as barrack blocks and radar stations. These were particularly dangerous jobs requiring low-level (fifty feet) flying and very accurate navigation.

A story we all had a good laugh over one evening was about the day the wing commander asked Harry and Ken to deliver a package for him to an air force station in Lancashire. Shortly before this request, Harry had been home on a forty-eight-hour pass and visited his uncle, who was the town clerk of Darwen. They came up with the bright idea of putting a decal of the town's coat of arms on the side of the Mosquito aircraft, "D-Dog." Not to be outdone, Ken obtained a decal for the Wigan coat of arms and had this put on the other side of the aircraft. When Ken and Harry landed to deliver the package, they were amazed to be greeted by a guard of honour led by an army major. Apparently, the major had been in the control tower as they came in to land. He had seen the coat of arms, assumed that royalty were arriving for a surprise visit, and decided to give them an appropriate welcome. The only such welcome they ever received in their lives, they hastened to tell us.

Another story we heard from Ken and Harry was about their squadron commander, Wing Commander Ivan Dale, DFC. Wing Commander Dale was affectionately known as "Daddy Dale," because he, a regular peacetime officer in the RAF, had now reached the venerable old age of forty years, considered quite ancient in the RAF in the era of World War II. Daddy did not usually do operational flying, but he liked to keep his hand in and would, on occasion, join the crews on their missions. This he did on a day when the squadron was programmed for an anti-movement patrol over the Ruhr.

Ken and Harry were flying over the North Sea at fifty feet (to avoid German radar) when Harry picked up a faint distress signal. "Mayday, Mayday!" Recognizing the voice he said, "My God, Ken, it's old Daddy!" Ken reacted immediately, taking his aircraft up to 7,000 feet—at risk to themselves—to improve radio transmission and try to get in touch with Daddy. They made the contact and Daddy told them he had lost an engine and was losing height rapidly. He had been trying to contact Dover. Ken and Harry now tried to relay his message to Dover; but as they attempted to do this they heard Daddy's last message, "I'm going in, chaps. Goodbye."

The two of them completed their mission and returned to base where at debriefing they reported the sad news about Daddy and his navigator.

Many years later, Harry discovered that Wing Commander Dale and Flight Lieutenant Hacket were buried in a war cemetery in Holland.

Daddy Dale's last words, "I'm going in, chaps, goodbye" were typically English, typically RAF and, I believe, typically Wing Commander Dale.

CHAPTER *20*

As Time Goes By

JUST OVER A YEAR after Mac returned to Canada, he received notification that he was to receive his Distinguished Flying Cross in Montreal from the governor general, Viscount Alexander. The investiture was to be held on a Sunday, so we booked a room in a hotel on Saturday night. At the hotel the parking attendant asked if we would need the car again that evening, because if so he would park it in a more easily available spot.

"No," we assured him. "We won't need it until tomorrow morning."

We had dinner, went up to our room and started to unpack. That morning Mac had asked me to put his things out on his bed and he would pack them. Suddenly, I heard a questioning voice. "Joan, where is my black tie?"

"I don't know," I replied. "I put it on the bed with your uniform. You packed your things."

PANIC. The tie was nowhere to be seen.

We went downstairs to the hotel gift shop. Did they have any black ties?

They did, but they all had dancing girls painted on them. Did they know where we could get one?

Well, there was an Army-Navy store somewhere in Verdun that stayed open late. Maybe there.

Out into the dark night we went. The parking attendant was not at all pleased to see us. "You said you would not need your car tonight," he sputtered. "You said . . ."

"It's an emergency," stated my husband with a grim face.

We drove around and around and finally found the store. They did have a black tie. We bought it just before they closed. We drove back to the hotel.

Our friendly parking attendant was waiting. "Will you need your car again tonight?"

"Absolutely not."

We went up to our room and started to get ready for bed. Mac picked up his neatly rolled pyjamas. Something fell from them onto the floor . . .

THE BLACK TIE!

The next day Viscount Alexander presented medals to the men in the three services, mostly army, in his usual very military way. His smiles were reserved for the three girls in the services who were receiving awards.

It was an exciting day.

On the way home, as we crossed the bridge the man at the toll booth took one look at Mac's uniform and said, "No charge."

Joan and Mac on the day he was awarded his DFC
JOAN MACDONALD

* * *

As time went on and our family grew—three children and two grandchildren—we were leading busy lives and sometimes did not even think of the air force for months at a time. Then, suddenly, something would jog our memories. A letter from an old air force friend, a phone call from one of Mac's crew, a Christmas card from someone we had not seen in years, and many memories would come flooding back.

One Christmas with the family coming home was such an occasion. Our house in the Eastern Townships of Quebec was shining and sparkling and ready for the holidays. Brilliant red poinsettias stood guard on each side of the white brick fireplace where striped red-and-white stockings for the grandchildren were hanging. A log fire crackled heartily, the snow was floating softly down, appetizing aromas drifted in from the kitchen mingling with the smell of fresh pine and flickering candles. Mac and I both heaved tired sighs and sat in the comfortable chairs in front of the fireplace to enjoy a well-earned eggnog. The children and grandchildren would be arriving shortly. Travel conditions were good with a full moon. The only thing left to do was to put the finishing touches to decorating the Scotch pine tree in front of the window in the living room.

Marcus, our aged golden retriever, lay sleeping in front of the fire. Suddenly his ears pricked up and his tale thumped on the floor. Some familiar-sounding cars were turning into the driveway. First to fly out of the cars were the grandchildren, followed by their parents; in the second car were our daughter and youngest son, who had travelled together from Boston. Soon the house was full of love and laughter, big hugs and kisses, giggles and squeals. Snowy jackets were shaken, boots pulled off, scarves and mittens hung up. This was the first time in years that everyone had been together for Christmas, so it was very special.

After supper the last part of the tree trimming was started. The grandchildren were given the silver foil icicles with the suggestion that they hang them on the tree separately, not just pitch them! I asked Mac if the icicles reminded him of anything. Without any hesitation he answered, "Yes, the window you used to decorate the tree in the WAAF sergeants' mess." The grandchildren were confused about how one could decorate a tree with windows, so Grandpa had to explain that "window" was the name for metal strips something like the icicles but bigger (twenty-five by five centimetres) and stronger. When the aircraft came to the places where the enemy night fighters would be, the strips of silver window would be dropped out of a chute; and as they floated down to earth they made blips on the German radar screens that looked as though hundreds of bombers were attacking at high speed. Also, the German night fighters flying through the window would have a screen filled with images of these pretend aircraft, and ground control could not give proper instructions to the pilots. It was that "window" that was hung on the Christmas tree all those years ago.

After tucking the sleepy grandchildren into bed, Mac and I looked out at the full moon shining reflected diamonds on the glittering snow.

"It's a bomber's moon," I said with a shiver.

"No, it's a Christmas moon," responded my husband, and I agreed that sounded much better.

CHAPTER 21

The Crew Reunion

76 Squadron—Home from Holme

Mac MacDonald's crew are required for a sortie—date 20th July to 24th July, 1985.

Target:	8 Mountain View, Stanstead, Quebec.
Time on Target:	Primary Target 6 p.m. 20th July.
Route:	Most direct
Intention:	To eat, drink and be merry and shoot a good line.
Call Sign:	Press on!

19th July— Arrive at MacDonald Base in Stanstead any time up to 2359 hrs for assignment to billets. To ensure nostalgia, stale buns and mouldy pork pies will be available.

20th July— Crew reunion and dinner at 6.00 p.m.

21st July— Alternate bomb aimer's target—dinner at Gil Baillargeon's in Sherbrooke.

22nd July—Stand down—Met forecast permitting, day by the pool for rest and relaxation. B.B.Q.

23rd July— The crew will survey the surrounding villages. Because of the shortage of tail lights, no bicycles will be issued. We suggest dinner at the Heermansmith Inn. After operations, tea and rum rations will be served on return to base.

24th July— Crew departs for destinations unknown.

R.S.V.P. to Sgt. Joan MacDonald, WAAF (retired).

IT WAS ABOUT FORTY YEARS after the war ended when we decided it would be a great idea to try to get the crew together for a special reunion. Sadly, Les Way, the navigator, had died several years before and Bill Lucas, the flight engineer from England, had major health problems and could not travel. Rick Bronson, the rear gunner, was unable to come because of business commitments, but the rest of the gang were there with their wives: the pilot, the wireless operator, the mid-upper gunner and the bomb-aimer—from British Columbia to Ontario to Quebec.

It was very good to get together again, to talk of those lonely nights flying through the dark and irate skies over Germany, and the contrast of playing darts, drinking beer, and singing songs around the old piano in the village pub; of leaves in London and excursions to Holme village; of all-ranks parties in the sergeant's mess; and nights when the old Halibag only just managed to make it back home.

One thing that was discussed, and in fact is often talked about when a group of aircrew who have flown in Halifaxes get together, is the "Lancaster syndrome." It seems that the press write so much about the Lancaster, and the public hear so much about it, that this aircraft overwhelms the Halifax; the Halifax story gets lost, much to the annoyance of the aircrew who regarded them as excellent aircraft—particularly the later models with the Hercules engines.

Over six thousand Halifaxes were built and they carried a bomb load of 13,000 lbs. They did not only serve in Bomber Command, but with Coastal and Transport Command, and they dropped supplies and agents into occupied Europe. The old warhorses, often called Halibags, also brought home many crews when they were so badly damaged that it was amazing they could still fly. Now, so many years later, the affection the aircrew and groundcrew have for their Halifaxes has resulted in two exciting projects, one on each side of the Atlantic.

The first project is completed: a mission to reconstruct a Halifax for the Yorkshire Air Museum in Elvington, Yorkshire, England. The second is the reconstruction of a Halifax at the Trenton Museum in Ontario, Canada. Both are very appropriate places—Yorkshire because so many aircrew flew their Halifaxes from the more than sixty airfields in the Yorkshire area, and Trenton because such a large proportion of the men who flew these Halifaxes were Canadians.

The British rebuilding of *Friday the Thirteenth* began in 1983. The proposed aircraft was named after the famous Halifax LV 907 that flew out of Lissett in Yorkshire with 158 Squadron. The original

Friday the Thirteenth completed an amazing 128 missions, more than any other Halifax. Unfortunately, like so many aircraft after the war, it was scrapped to provide the metal for pots and pans.

Eager volunteers now looked for parts for the new *Friday the Thirteenth* all over Europe, following stories of where aircraft had crashed and checking archives. They wanted to find as many original Halifax parts as possible. The biggest find was in 1985 when a section of a crashed Halifax fuselage about twenty feet long was located on the Isle of Lewis in the Outer Hebrides. Jock McKenzie, a local crofter, had been using it as a "hen hut." The chairman of the Yorkshire Air Museum arranged to have the piece of fuselage airlifted to England where volunteers at British Aerospace restored it before it was incorporated into the rebuilding by other volunteers.

After more than a decade, *Friday the Thirteenth* was completed and on Friday, September 13, 1996—which by a great coincidence was also my husband's birthday—a ceremony was held at Elvington as a salute to a great wartime aircraft and a memorial to the brave men who flew it. More than six thousand people were present at the "roll-out" from the hangar. It looked like a brand-new aircraft. No one would have known that thirteen years had been spent using parts gathered from wreckage and carefully put together.

Bill and Mac inspect *Friday the Thirteenth* at Elvington Museum, 1994   JOAN MACDONALD

Air Chief Marshal Sir Michael Knight unveiled the Halifax and with him was the first man to fly the original *Friday the Thirteenth* in 1944, Pilot Officer Joe Hitchman from Sheffield. He must have been a very proud man that day.

Meanwhile, not quite all of the original *Friday the Thirteenth* had been designated for the scrap heap. Someone had saved the bomb-bedecked nose panel, and this was displayed at the RAF Museum at Hendon, with an explanation of the history of this aircraft.

Halifax LV 907 joined Lissett on March 10, 1944, with the letter "F." This was rather a dubious honour because no aircraft with that letter had ever completed a tour, and eight Halifaxes bearing the letter "F" had been lost in the last twelve months. The insignia painted on "F" was unusual and was obviously done by someone with a macabre sense of humour! They included an upside-down horseshoe, a ladder across the entry door, a broken mirror and a skull and crossbones. At one time a large white tombstone was painted on the nose with all the crews' names on it, but this had to be taken off because it shone in the searchlights. A scythe, dripping with blood, was painted around a skull and crossbones with the quote, "As ye sow so shall ye reap. 1944–194*."

As *Friday the Thirteenth* miraculously continued to survive each operation, the bomb load on the nose was extended. A key was added for the twenty-first operation. Later awards added were a DFC and a DFM; after eighty operations a DSO; and the hundredth operation rated a VC.

One piece of information tells a touching story. *Friday the Thirteenth* achieved a very unusual distinction among Bomber Command Halifaxes. It actually survived long enough to require a major inspection.

* * *

The story of the Halifax reconstruction at Trenton, Ontario, is also a fascinating one. On April 23, 1945, Halifax NA 337 flew out of Tarrant Rushton airfield in England on a mission to drop supplies to a Norwegian resistance group. It was a relatively new aircraft, only on its fifth mission.

The supplies had just been dropped when the aircraft veered off course and was hit by German anti-aircraft fire from a battery at Minnesund Bridge. The round pierced the bottom of the wing, setting one of the starboard engines on fire and causing the pilot to ditch on Lake Mjøsa, about 110 kilometres north of Oslo. Although the crew of six (British) survived the crash, five of them died of hypothermia in the frigid lake. The only survivor was Thomas Weightman, the tail gunner.

In 1994 a group of veterans formed The Halifax Aircraft Association in Toronto. The president was Jeff Jeffery, a Halifax pilot of thirty-two missions, who stated that the association had a goal to restore a Halifax as a permanent memorial to Canadian veterans, to be on exhibition for future generations.

Mr. Jeffery's group found their Halifax through Karl Kjarsgaard, a Halifax buff and a pilot for Canadian Airlines who had already helped the Yorkshire Air Museum in their search for parts for *Friday the Thirteenth*.

Mr. Kjarsgaard had heard of two Norwegians who had a lead on some Halifax parts and he asked for a meeting with them. At the meeting he was offered the salvage rights to a whole aircraft and a sonar map of its location. The plane was NA 337 and it was 225 metres below the surface of Lake Mjøsa. One of the Norwegians at the meeting was Tore Marsoe, who, at sixteen years of age, heard the German guns open fire and saw a low-flying plane pass over his farmhouse on the night of April 23, 1945.

Veterans Affairs gave a grant of $100,000 to help Dacon Industry Inspeksjon AS of Norway in July 1995 to recover the Halifax in a very high-tech operation using a minisub and a custom-built crane dubbed "The Moby Grip." NA 337 eventually surfaced on September 3, 1995, and the Canadian Forces sent a twelve-member crew with four transport planes to clean, crate, and fly the Halifax back to her new home. The sole survivor, Mr. Weightman, was presented with his old coffee thermos found intact in his turret.

Mr. Jeffery says the object is to have every piece of the aircraft restored to working order, a daunting task made more so by the plane's obsolescence and the fact that there is no pool of spare parts. The project has a workforce of 112 keen volunteers.

There is an interesting connection between the two projects of rebuilding a Halifax on both sides of the Atlantic. Both groups used some fuselage from a crashed Halifax from the Island of Lewis, and both pieces of wreckage had been utilized as a "henhouse" for many years. The wreckage used by the Trenton group was owned by Mary MacDonald, who used it at her home in Grimshadar.

According to *The Halibag News*—a newsletter from Trenton—the wreckage came from a Halifax from 518 Squadron diverted to Stornoway on the Island of Lewis. Returning from a meteorological flight, this aircraft landed on a wet runway under adverse weather conditions and ran off the end of the runway into the "drink." The aircraft was quickly recovered, but it was damaged beyond repair and was sold to the local scrapyard.

The Halifax rescued from a Norwegian lake   *BILL BATEMAN*

CHAPTER 22

Resolute

FOR MAC AND ME, 1989 was the year our lives started to change drastically and forever; the year when we were called upon to use all the skills of courage and faith we had learned throughout the war; the year we were challenged to deal, once again, with a crisis that was like another operational mission for both of us.

Mac had been chosen to be a district governor for Rotary International and for many months, following a ten-day training session at Nashville, Tennessee—which was a learning experience without parallel—we had travelled to all the Rotary clubs in Mac's district in Quebec, Vermont and New Hampshire, as he carried out his duties. Towards the end of his year of office he hosted a conference at the Chateau Bromont in the Eastern Townships of Quebec. It was a busy and successful event, and we were now looking forward to a rest, a holiday, and our return to living at a somewhat quieter pace.

Then one day I noticed a small red spot on Mac's back, which we decided to have checked. I won't go through all the weeks of misdiagnosis, of being told it was nothing to worry about, of finally receiving the diagnosis of pemphigus vulgaris, a rare and strange disease that is as horrible as it sounds. I won't go into details about the seven months that Mac was in hospital and I stayed at the hospital hotellerie, being in his room practically every day from seven a.m. to seven p.m.; the major surgeries; the transformation of an athletic, vital, energetic man to someone who could barely walk or eat.

In the midst of all the problems, Mac, whose resistance was nil and whose immune system was wrecked, developed an eye infection in both eyes that could not be stopped; and in a few weeks he was totally and permanently blind.

There is a strange phenomenon that happens sometimes when people go blind. Like someone who has lost a limb but can still feel the pain in the nerves of the lost arm or leg, a newly blind person is sometimes convinced that he or she can see. One night Mac was totally convinced that he could see his partner in the next hospital bed and when I came for my usual morning visit he told me he had seen the clock on the wall last night and it was at midnight. One of the hardest things I ever had to do was to tell him there was no clock on the wall.

I remember going to the hospital chapel and praying to God not to let my husband lose his sight; and then later, I remember, going to the chapel and praying God would give me the strength to deal with what was happening so we could still, somehow, continue our happy life together.

I remember thinking, at this time, of all the trips we made for Rotary when we would come home and Mac would look out our living room window at the beautiful sunsets and say, "That was a good visit but it's always good to see the hills of home." I sobbed my heart out, knowing he would never see those hills again.

So this is a story of blindness, of how Mac coped with that blindness and how he developed the light from within.

I never doubted that our 76 Squadron motto, "Resolute," was an appropriate motto for us personally. I had watched Mac take off and waited for him to return from many missions, always wondering if he would return; and now I was sure we could work together to overcome any obstacles. Not that we were perfect—far from it. There were times when Mac was in despair about this black world he had to live in; and there were times when I was so totally exhausted I thought I would scream if he asked me to do one thing more.

We came home from the hospital in the summer of 1990. Mac was so weak that he had to be pushed from one room to another in a wheelchair. But we were home. One of the doctors suggested we go to a convalescent hospital for therapy for a couple of months, but we said no. We would do it ourselves. Our family was coming, the sun was shining, and Mac would be eating my cooking. Somehow we would get the help we needed. We promised ourselves that if we still needed the convalescent home in September, then we would go; but after all the months in hospital we wanted this summer at home first.

Mac could not see the sunsets but I could describe them to him. He could hear our pet chipmunk chattering on the patio in the early morning, hear the rain on the roof, smell the lavender and the wild roses in the garden. He could chat with the neighbours, sit and have a drink by the pool in the evenings, and listen to the songs of the birds. True, his vision was gone, but his inner vision was still strong. Our house and our village would be his healing ground.

We built a ramp for Mac so his wheelchair could move easily into the garden. We found a wonderful girl to help him. She had an outrageous sense of humour and made him laugh. We discovered a young man living near to us who had just graduated as a physical therapist and who was delighted to help with the exercises. Most of all, Mac's determination took over. Each day he walked a few more steps. Each day he added one more exercise. Each day he gained a little more strength. The day he walked to the end of our driveway was a red-letter day. Then, each day, he added one more house on our street to his walk. I had a strong feeling that if I could just get him into the swimming pool and start him swimming it would be the best thing in the world, but how to do it—how to get him down the steep ladder on the side of the pool? Then, one day when all our family was home, Mac announced that with a little help he could and would get into that pool. With the assistance of two or three members of the family he was soon standing in the shallow end. Everyone cheered. Someone fetched a bottle of champagne. Then we started to laugh. We had been so busy working on getting him into the pool that we had never thought about what to do next or how hard it would be to get him out!

However, he managed a few slow strokes and was then half pulled, half lifted out of the pool and that was the beginning of our daily swim.

As he became stronger we received a lot of help from various organizations. People came to teach him how to walk with a white cane, how to walk properly with a sighted guide, how to find the way around the house without bumping into things. The people who came to help were young, enthusiastic, no-nonsense. They did not encourage pity. They did encourage self-help and the use of aids that were available. There were books on tape, Braille instruction, and eventually a Braille typewriter and playing cards. There were cooking lessons—not a favourite with Mac. He had never liked working in the kitchen and was not about to change now! There was an electronic talking calculator, a talking watch, a beeper to tell when you had poured three-quarters of a cup full of liquid.

We learned many things about blindness. We learned that children instinctively seemed to know the right things to do. My brother's five-year-old grandson was told that Uncle Mac could not see, so we must be careful not to leave boots and toys around in case he might trip over them. The next day Johnathan came home from kindergarten with some leaves stuck on a piece of paper. He showed them to everyone but then went over to Mac, took his hand and said, "Here Uncle Mac, feel my leaves."

When Mac was out walking by himself one day, a little girl from across the street came up to him and said, "Hello, Mr. MacDonald, I'm Sarah," and chatted as they walked together for a while. Some adults are not so perceptive and don't say who they are. It is difficult to recognize voices, particularly as Mac has a hearing problem, too.

Sarah, seeing one of our friends coming to read to Mac every Tuesday afternoon, asked if she could read to him too. Of course he was delighted. Sarah picked out a book about hockey because she knew that Mac had coached junior hockey teams at one point and she not only read it with great feeling but also described the pictures in the book with enthusiasm.

Our grandchildren were great. When Mac was learning how to eat neatly, our ten-year-old grandson kept a good eye on things. He would say in a reassuring tone of voice, "Bada, you have lost a piece of steak, I'll fix it for you." And they discovered it was just as easy to give a big hug to someone who could not see.

When we had been home from the hospital for a few months, Mac decided he wanted to have a party. I said, "Okay, we'll invite eight people for dinner," thinking this was a good beginning. "No, no," said my ambitious husband, "I want a big party like we used to have, a party for forty or fifty people." Then he remarked, "You know, some people who have not seen me since I became blind are not going to know how to handle it. Remember years ago when we had our Hawaiian party and we made tags for all the ladies with their names translated into Hawaiian? I think I'll do the ladies' names in Braille this time." It worked. Everyone was so intrigued and busy trying to figure out her name that there were no awkward moments at all.

Another landmark in dealing with blindness was when Mac decided he wanted to try cross-country skiing again. He and our eldest son tried it first on the back lot in the winter of 1992. Mac was always a good skier and he hadn't forgotten a thing. They came in rosy cheeked and laughing, and that was the beginning of regular cross-country skiing. A girl who came to work for us and who became like a daughter to us took Mac skiing when conditions were good. They skied at a nearby area of wide and well-groomed trails where they could ski side by side. Mac wore a sign that said "Blind Skier," so that people would understand if he did not get out of the way. As other skiers went by they would call out, "Bravo!" and there were many smiles.

John and Mac cross-country skiing   JOAN MACDONALD

That same winter Mac wanted to go back to Hawaii, our favourite place in the world. I was afraid it would be too hard to do, that he would feel too bad about not being able to see his favourite things over there, but he did not feel that way at all. He wanted to walk on the beach and listen to the ocean, to get away from the winter and swim in the huge pool at the complex. He wanted all the children to come and share our holidays with us. We went back to Maui and it was a great success. The children came in turns and with some overlapping. We did special things with all of them and had a wonderful holiday. However, there were always new things to learn! Travelling was made much better by the helpful airline staff, but the main challenge on those very long flights was getting into the tiny toilets in the aircraft. Mac had difficulties finding things for himself and I understood that because I had the same problem in the little broom closets, so we managed to squeeze in there together and came out to walk back to our seats with rather red faces.

When we were travelling in England and Scotland with my brother John and his wife Mary, John was in charge of Mac for going to the men's room. One day we were in a very pretentious restaurant with lots of heavy, carved wood and red velvet curtains. Mac and John made their routine trip and came out of there laughing hilariously.

Apparently when they were "in position," John had said, "Okay, Mac, fire at will," whereupon a very large man at the other end of the room rushed immediately and noisily out of the door.

John said, "I think he thinks we are the Mafia."

Mac said, "No—I think his name is Will!"

So there was still laughter and joy in our lives in spite of all the problems; and once again we had emphasized the true meaning of our squadron motto, "Resolute."

CHAPTER 23

Yes, You Can Go Holme Again

IT WAS A VERY SMALL notice in the Canadian *Legion* magazine. Just a few words, but our response was immediate and enthusiastic. "Possible reunion for 76 Squadron in September 1992," I read to my husband. "For further information contact Mrs. Reed." This was followed by an address in York.

Seventy-six Squadron—York—Yorkshire—England. Exciting days! Our thoughts flew back in time, tumbling over each other with mixed memories. Happiness and terror, laughter and tragedy, a nostalgic combination of reflections about life and love while stationed on a bleak bomber base on the Yorkshire Moors.

I wrote at once to the unknown Mrs. Reed, explaining that my husband, Flight Lieutenant Malcolm MacDonald, DFC, and I, Sergeant Joan Hemingway, WAAF, had both served with 76 Squadron at Holme on Spalding Moor during World War II and we would like to hear more about the reunion.

Then came the big surprise. Mrs. Reed, on opening the letter, squealed to her husband, "It's Joan! It's Joan! It's Joan and Mac!"

Mrs. Reed, whose married name I had not known, was a fellow WAAF sergeant and a good friend, Paddy Welborn. We had shared a Nissen hut for years on our bomber base, but had lost touch with each other since 1945. Soon we were on the phone spanning the Atlantic and making plans for our coming meeting at the Knavesmire in York on September 11. So this small notice in *Legion* magazine eventually led to two visits to England, two 76 Squadron reunions and a

WAAF Sgt. "Paddy" (Welborn) Reed

PADDY REED

84

variety of reminiscences and memories that will forever be in our hearts.

September 11, 1992. Mac and I are walking down a narrow street, The Shambles, in York. It is as though we have never left there. For one brief, shining moment we are in air force uniform, strolling along hand in hand, deciding to go to Betty's Bar, our favourite hangout, for a drink. The memories are so vivid I would not have been at all surprised to run into some of Mac's crew or my WAAF sergeant friends from Holme on Spalding Moor.

Then a jet aircraft streaks across the sky and breaks the spell. It is too modern, it should have been a Halifax with four engines, and four propellers whirling, as 76 Squadron takes off over York on yet another operational mission.

But we discovered, "Yes, you can go Holme again": back to 76 Squadron reunions, back to the ancient and historical city of York with so many memories for us. We visited the Station Hotel, much more sophisticated than during the war years, but happily remembered as the place where we had our first date. Mac's blindness did not deter him. He remembered where everything was and I remembered how everything happened. It was a wonderful experience. We were back in our favourite beautiful city surrounded by its Roman walls, walking along its tiny cobbled streets, looking in the windows of the fascinating shops displaying delicate china and crystal, checking out the bookstores loaded with air force novels and histories. We rediscovered Betty's Bar, which is now Betty's Tea Room, but still displays air force memorabilia. There are crew photos and six hundred signatures scratched on mirrors by airmen from all over the world.

In York Minster, the Astronomical Clock, a memorial to eighteen thousand fallen airmen, stands proudly in the north transept. One side of the memorial represents day and night and the movement of the sun in the heavens throughout the year; the other is a dial of the night skies of the northern hemisphere through which our airmen flew their perilous missions, with the constellations in perpetual motion according to their times and seasons.

The words above the Roll of Honour were: *They went through the air and space without fear, and the shining stars marked their shining deeds.*

The most exciting part of the reunions was rediscovering old friends we had not seen for so many years. The flags of Norway, Australia, New Zealand, Canada and Britain were displayed at the head table, reminding us all of the time when men from these countries, and others, were flying on operations together. The comradeship of long ago was still there.

My special moment was meeting Paddy again. With a big hug and a few tears we were soon giggling about our life in the Nissen hut and our adventures on the base. We knew without a doubt that we would have known each other anywhere and bemoaned the fact that we could not find more WAAF sergeants to join in our happiness.

Another person we were delighted to meet was Squadron Leader John Crampton, DFC, AFC, who proposed the toast to 76 Squadron at the 1992 reunion dinner. We remembered Squadron Leader Crampton, often known as "Big John" because of his 6'6" height, as an excellent flight commander at Holme on Spalding Moor while Mac was doing his tour of operations. We also remembered the time that Group Captain Pelly-Fry "stopped the war" for an hour while he and Squadron Leader Crampton, two enthusiastic aeromodellers, took to the runway with one of John's model aircraft.

More recently—in fact, in 1999—we heard of the squadron leader's exploits with the permanent air force back in the 1950s,

Squadron Leader John Crampton proposes the toast to 76 Squadron   JOAN MacDONALD

adventures that had been kept under wraps for many years. Squadron Leader Crampton commanded a special flight of American RB-45C reconnaissance aircraft in the 1950s in two highly secret assignments when he checked the Soviet air defences during the cold war. His logbook showed these assignments as "Practise Recon.," but in reality they were high-risk flights extremely important to the security of the West. Again reason for much pride in the exploits of another 76 Squadron flight commander.

One of our most enjoyable experiences when we returned to England was a telephone conversation with Group Captain James Pelly-Fry. Even after more than fifty years had passed, I must confess I was still a little in awe of him, remembering the station commander and the WAAF sergeant!

I said, "I'm not sure whether I should call you 'Sir.'"

He laughed and said, "James sounds much better." The three of us had a most interesting conversation, followed by some great correspondence after we returned home. His letters were always signed "James P.F.," written in green ink (a green endorsement was a sign of air force approval—in other words, one had not put up any blacks!).

James had a totally fascinating life, mainly as a "contented airman." He was selected as personal assistant to Arthur Harris, then air commodore, in Palestine in 1938 and the relationship between the two men continued throughout the war years. He also spent a year living in Buckingham Palace as air equerry to King George VI, which provided him with insight into the lives of the royal family, for whom he had a great admiration.

A different era of his career was when he was with 88 Squadron taking part in operations over France, including the Dieppe raid, flying Douglas Boston light bombers. His squadron established a warm relationship with their fighter escorts, and the wing leader would call "Hi-de-hi!" to the fighter pilots, who would respond enthusiastically, "Pelly-Fry!"

In 1994, Group Captain Pelly-Fry's excellent book *Heavenly Days* was published. He had promised to write a few words on our copy but, sadly, this was not to be. Instead we received a note from his daughter-in-law explaining that James had died on December 6th. He was having a celebration lunch with his publisher and two friends when he collapsed, was taken to hospital and died peacefully and painlessly a few hours later. Anna said it was such a relief that he lived to see the book published. We were happy about this also, but wished he could have had a little more time to hear from all of the friends who would be contacting him about *Heavenly Days*.

James had dedicated his book to his late wife, saying, "To my darling Arleen who gave me such a blissfully long and happy married life and encouraged me to write these memoirs. Now she can read all these pages again in heaven."

Now we hope they can read the pages in heaven together.

September 3, 1994. We are staying at the same hotel as Bill and Gaye Bateman. As our contact for many years has been limited to Christmas cards, we are delighted to join them, together with other aircrew and their wives. "Shooting a line" is not unknown as the wine flows and many memories are awakened.

At the reunion dinner everyone wanted to say hello to Group Captain "Hank" Iveson. His popularity was obvious as he chatted with his crews of long ago. Unfortunately he was very ill, but he had made a special effort to be present. "Resolute" was the motto as usual.

Going out to the old airfield was an essential part of the weekend and we all walked around with our special memories, looking for the places we used to know so well. The officers' mess was still standing. I saw the building where I used to work. I looked down the crumbling hallway, thinking of the Intelligence Room, the Teleprinter Section, the W/T area—hives of activity in the old days. The dark piles of rubble in the corridor did not encourage further exploration. Outside was an old bicycle rack where we used to park our issue bicycles when we came on duty. I wondered whatever had happened to dear old 301.

The Batemans and the MacDonalds at the reunion, 1994   BILL BATEMAN

At eleven o'clock we gathered just past the guardhouse and admired the memorial to the members of 76 Squadron killed in action. Wreaths were laid in memory of friends or relatives. It was a quiet and emotional time.

Afterwards we drove down to the village and to the WAAF site, passing the bend in the road where Mac and I had escaped the police who were checking for tail lights! The field opposite the WAAF site over which we cycled to main camp to go on duty looked exactly the same. It was a very nostalgic moment. Back in the village we had lunch at the Cross Keys Pub, remembering the evenings we spent there drinking beer and/or gin and limes. Several squadron photos were displayed on the wall.

The Parish Church of All Saints, better known to the squadron airmen and airwomen during the war as "The Little Church on the Hill," was our next destination. The church was particularly remembered by the aircrews who, when returning from operations, saw the red warning light on top of the tower, which also served as a homing beacon for them.

"The Little Church on the Hill"
BILL BATEMAN

We were welcomed to All Saints by the Rev. David Cook, and the tiny church was soon filled to capacity with air force personnel and their families from all over the world. The mayor and the mace-bearer emphasized the English traditions and their pride in those traditions; and members of the 76 Squadron Association Committee read the lessons and took part in the service. The special prayers for the air force were beautiful:

> O Almighty God, who makes the clouds your chariots, and walks on the wings of the wind: Govern, we pray, the officers, men, and women of the Royal Air Force in all their operations and flights in the service of their country; guide and guard them, both in the paths of the air and in the ways of righteousness; through Jesus Christ, our Lord. Amen.

The Service of Dedication and Remembrance held on September 4, 1994, was one we will always remember. As the congregation sang "O Valiant Hearts," the clergy and the officers of 76 Squadron Association moved to the north aisle for the dedication and unveiling of a beautiful memorial to the members of 76 Squadron. killed in action in World War II—a two-light stained glass window designed with great flair and imagination by Ann Southeran of York.

The prayer of dedication was given:

> Bless O Lord the images and symbols here depicted in Thy House, that after ages may learn from them of the sacrifice made by the men and women of the Royal Air Force during World War II, in particular the members of 76 Squadron stationed nearby. May the light of Thy world illuminate our path through life and bring us safely to Thy eternal kingdom as, in the dark days of the war, this House was a beacon and a known way.

> Let us remember before God those who have died for their country in war, those whom we knew, and those whose memory we treasure, and all those who have lived and died in the service of mankind.

> In their honour we solemnly dedicate these memorial windows.

The window was then unveiled by Group Captain Douglas Iveson, DSO, DFC, squadron commander of 76 Squadron (RAF) from November 1943 to August 1944. We all agreed there could be no more appropriate person to do the honours than Group Captain (Hank) Iveson.

The glowing new window is directly above another special memorial from the 76 Squadron Association, the Book of Remembrance. This book, bound in blue leather and tooled in gold, contains the names of our comrades killed in action. The names were written by a calligraphist on vellum and the book is kept in a glass-topped oak desk on an oak stand, both of which were carved and donated by George Woods, a cabinetmaker who served with 76 Squadron ground crew.

One name in this Book of Remembrance has a unique story—that of Dorothy Robson. In October 1937, Dorothy went up to Leeds University to read for a degree in physics, an unusual ambition in those pre-war days. She graduated with a bachelor of science degree in the summer of 1940. Dorothy then tried to join the WAAF but her petite form was considered too short and she was rejected. Eventually she was accepted to work as a scientist with the Ministry of Aircraft Production, joining the team of Prof. R.H.S. Blackett and Dr. Braddick, who were developing the secret Mark XIV bombsight. Dorothy realized that the bombsight would be even more effective if always correctly installed and if the bomb aimers on the squadrons were more expertly informed. To this end, she became a regular visitor to bomber airfields in Yorkshire and Lincolnshire, doing air tests whenever possible, especially in new aircrafts where she could check installation and calibration. The aircrews all enjoyed her, calling her "The Girl with the Laughing Eyes," or sometimes "Bombsight Bertha."

She was at Holme on Spalding Moor a week before her twenty-fourth birthday and did an air test with Flight Lieutenant Jimmy Steel's crew in a new aircraft that was supposed to make its first operational flight that night. The navigator of the crew stood down to allow Dorothy to take his place in the nose of the Halifax.

No one knows exactly what happened, but not long after takeoff on a misty November morning, Flight Lieutenant Steele's aircraft crashed in high ground near Market Weighton. Three of the crew were killed instantly, the mid-upper gunner was dead on admission to hospital, and the pilot and rear gunner died the following day. Dorothy, grievously injured, lived for just one more day. Dorothy had asked her father, if anything like this happened, to have her ashes scattered from the air, and this was done.

Because she was not a member of the armed forces, her death was not formally marked by any medals or memorials, but her name is in our Book of Remembrance, a well-earned tribute to the girl who, like the men she flew with, gave her all.

After the service in our little church on the hill, the congregation all took their turns in examining and admiring the newly revealed window. Everyone, I am sure, had their own poignant memories of those long-ago days and nights represented by the images and symbols set in the glowing glass.

Memories of my life as a WAAF sergeant serving with 76 Squadron came flooding back, and as I described the window to Mac we shared our thoughts on this memorable day, both agreeing that the story of the Squadron was well told. (A detailed description of the window can be found in Appendix D.)

The images and the symbols—76 Squadron memorial window
RAF 76 SQUADRON ASSOCIATION

CHAPTER 24

Ken Mason's Story

OF ALL THE EVENTS that happened when we returned to England for the reunions, one was overwhelming. Mac and I had often talked about Woolfy and his crew when R-Roger was shot down over St. Vith on Boxing Day of 1944; and we had heard no news of any survivors.

As we took our places at the table for the reunion dinner, a man walked over to Mac, hand outstretched. It was Ken Mason from Niagara Falls, Canada, the mid-upper gunner and only surviving member of R-Roger.

Ken had an amazing story to tell that night, which he later wrote for the Squadron newsletter.

While the remaining crews of 76 Squadron were returning from their raid on St. Vith and were later being diverted to other stations, young (nineteen years old) Ken Mason, the mid-upper gunner of R-Roger, was going through a terrifying experience. Ken was a member of a crew of eight, one more than usual because a mid-under gunner was flying with them.

There was bitter fighting on the ground as the American and British armies tried to stem the 5th SS Panzers in atrocious midwinter conditions. The Panzers were following Hitler's orders to thrust towards Antwerp.

The defending flak was extremely heavy and R-Roger was hit by an 88 shell that exploded in the wireless operator's compartment. Ari Clarke was blown to bits, George Floyd and Ralph Emmerson were both killed, and the pilot, Woolf, was terribly injured. The control panel and rudder pedals were gone. Woolf told the flight engineer, Jack Gray, to tell the rest of the crew to bail out. Woolf, Smith, Mason, Gray and Newton bailed out, the pilot through the hole caused by the explosion when the nose of the aircraft started to break away. He drifted quite a long way from the other boys.

Ken landed in a huge tree, his feet dangling six feet from the ground. The others were in the brush about 500 yards away. As they parachuted down they saw about three hundred German troops in box formation coming for them. There were over a million German troops in the area and about 1,200 tanks.

Thinking quickly, Ken ran towards the troops and found a pile of brush in a swale by a logging road and managed to wriggle under the brush without the Germans spotting him. He then heard three shots, which indicated that the enemy had shot Smith, Gray and Newton.

The Germans began a further search, going back and forth through the woods, many times just missing Ken. They brought in more troops and swept through the brush six feet apart. Once, a sergeant stood right beside Ken, his pistol held loosely in his hand unconsciously aimed at Ken's head, but did not see him. Eventually, in the pitch darkness, they gave up and left. Ken sat on the mud road, wondering what he should do. He was exhausted but unable to try to sleep. In the morning he decided he would head towards Luxembourg, because he assumed the Germans would probably be looking for him if he headed for the American lines. He walked ten miles into the woods and found a hunter's cabin where he rested and studied his map.

About a quarter of a mile south of the cabin was a paved road that branched off into the main road leading to Luxembourg. Ken followed this road to an intersection that was seething with military police, troop transports and guns. He took a chance by crossing the road and reversing direction, heading, according to his map, to Liège. He walked for several hours and was extremely hungry, so decided to look for a farmhouse. He did find an abandoned garden and ate some frozen carrots and cabbages, then returned to the brush by the side of the highway, found a protected spot, and fell asleep. In the morning he found a farmhouse tucked off to the side of the highway, but the farmer and his wife were talking to some soldiers, so he decided to wait until it was dark again to look for food.

After dark he went into the henhouse and found a couple of eggs, and had some squirts of milk from the cow in the shed; but when a dog started to bark he put some distance between the farm and himself and once again holed up for the night.

Next day Ken pressed on again. He saw a German dispatch rider on a motorbike heading down the road and about two hours later a German staff car stopped close to where he was hiding in the brush. The four high-ranking officers in the car, he found out later, were Von

Rundstedt, Keitel, Kesselring and Jodl. They had stopped for a smoke break. After they left, Ken resumed his journey, going deeper into the brush and keeping the highway on his left and a small, paved road on the right. There were signs of American troops having been in one area and also a sign tacked to a tree stating: "You are now in British territory. Anyone seen moving will be shot without warning." There was a small village behind Ken on the road that angled off the highway and he decided to investigate it. This, he found out later, was a big mistake.

After several near run-ins with the Germans again (during the day he was saved from being recognized because he was wearing his brown inner flying suit), he was finally challenged as he crossed a ploughed field. Twice he did not answer the challenge and kept going but when about fifty soldiers with rifles and machine guns showed themselves, he stuck up his hands and said, "RAF."

He was stripped naked in the snow. They took his flying suit, his sweater and an extra pair of socks. They said, "For you, the war is over." A frightened and frozen Ken was put in the back of a personnel carrier and taken to a house on the edge of the village where there were about nine soldiers, the lady of the house, and two children. The lady handed Ken a coffee but a soldier came down hard on the back of his hand with a rifle butt. He was all for sticking Ken right there but the others pushed him off.

At about 0700 hours Ken was taken to another house, which was guarded inside and out. There were the four high-ranking officers he had seen on the highway, with many other officers. He was caught in the sector commanded by Jodl in the German front lines, and was in the headquarters of the German offensive. Ken was interrogated and Jodl ordered him to be shot. He was taken outside. There was a brick wall around the back yard and six riflemen waited with rifles on their laps. An *Oberleutnant* with a black bandana told Ken to come.

Just then, an American jeep pulled into the back yard with two men aboard, the driver and someone standing holding the top of the windshield. Everyone immediately jumped to attention, clicked heels and saluted the obviously high-ranking officer.

The officer held up his hand and walked over to Ken, who, realizing that this guy was a "big wheel," showed no fear, came to attention and said, "Good Morning, Sir!"

The officer responded, asking, "How old are you?"

Ken lied and said, "I'm seventeen, Sir."

He asked, "How long have you been down?" Ken told him.

The officer said, "You must be hungry, it's well into January," to which Ken replied, "I'm starving."

The officer went inside the building where some loud talk took place. He then came out and said, "We are going to send you back with some of your English and American friends."

Ken said, "Thank you very much, Sir," and the officer took off.

He was a tall man, about six feet two inches, khaki uniform with a forage cap and no insignia, hair short and sandy, flecked with grey. Whoever this high-ranking German officer was, he arrived just in time to use his authority and save Ken's life.

Ken was then transported to a farmhouse to get something to eat. A major in the *Wermacht* talked to him and got him a hot bowl of soup. After two more stays in different houses he was eventually taken by truck to a church on the outskirts of Prom in Luxembourg. Here he was taken to the top floor. A door opened and there were a couple of steps down into a room. A gun butt was smacked into the back of his head and he went sprawling onto the wounded leg of an American glider pilot. There were seventy-nine prisoners, including Ken and an Aussie air gunner. Many of the prisoners were seriously wounded and had been for a week with no food or medical attention.

The next morning everyone who was deemed capable of working was told they would have to work at night on a rail siding to get supplies to the front. One morning they were all lined up to be counted when a squadron of Thunderbolts strafed and rocketed them, hitting a lot of the men. In the afternoon the Thunderbolts came back and attacked the church, killing twenty-nine Germans who were eating supper.

After this the prisoners were moved out to Koblenz where the two gunners were separated from the army personnel. They spent a night in a marquee on frozen ground and then were marched to Frankfurt by Hitler Youth, where they were separated.

After this, Ken spent five days in a boxcar on the way to a prisoner-of-war camp in Barth on the Baltic. He was very ill with pneumonia and dysentery and only weighed about seventy pounds. It took him a long time to recover from his capture and his stay in the camp.

After the war, the bodies of Woolf, Newton, Grey and Smith were all exhumed for reburial. They all had bullet holes in their skulls behind their right ear.

Before Ken and his wife attended the 76 Squadron Reunion they visited the gravesites of all of his crew. Ken said they were a great bunch of guys and he thinks of them often.

Ken Mason tells Mac his story

CHAPTER 25

The Light from Within

ANDY ROONEY ONCE OBSERVED, "It is paradoxical that the idea of living a long life appeals to everyone, but the idea of getting old doesn't appeal to anyone." Still, now that Mac and I are in our twilight years, we often find pleasure in looking back at our time wearing the light blue of the Royal Canadian Air Force and the Women's Auxiliary Air Force. Long ago and far away for sure, but still clearly remembered, even though our memories may fault us on some details.

The richest source of insight is from those who actually fought the war; they tell it like it was.

* * *

In 1995 we were adjusting to our new way of life and Mac's blindness and doing well. We were travelling, visiting our children, and being involved in many activities.

Then, one night, in May 1995, Mac suffered a stroke and a severe seizure. He lost his ability to speak and for a while was unable to recognize us. It was a nightmare, but thanks to prompt medical attention, the support of our family and Mac's own valiant spirit, he came through a second severe illness. He worked hard on speech therapy, gradually built up his walks every day and eventually even cross-country skied again. Unfortunately, he had lost all he had learned about Braille, but there was not time for everything and it was more important to learn to talk properly again. He never lost his sense of humour and we never, ever, heard him ask, "Why me?"

The light from within shone again and although he was more limited in what he could do, he still managed to lead a meaningful life and set an example for all of us.

During these physically and emotionally trying times, I often thought of the words of one of the surgeons who tried to comfort me back in 1990. I told him, "Now we have to go home and learn to live with the blindness."

"Yes, Mrs. MacDonald," he replied, "but you must realize it is almost a miracle that he is here at all." And I knew he was right.

When we were leaving the hospital for the second time the ambulance driver asked, "Where are we going to, Mrs. MacDonald?" I was surprised that he would ask that question.

"Well, home of course," I replied. "Where else would we go?"

During the long recovery period, I found that writing was one way to keep myself occupied with an interesting project of my own. There is nothing more encouraging than seeing oneself in print! Following the old adage, "Write about what you know," I concentrated on the period of World War II and was soon published in several magazines, such as *Legion*, *World War II*, *Living History*, *Western People*, etc., and I have used some of the material from these articles in this book.

In December 1998, *The Rotarian* magazine published my article "The Light from Within," my story of living with blindness, and it was illustrated with a photograph of Mac and me taken on the day he was awarded his Distinguished Flying Cross. He was, of course, in his air force uniform. The article brought an incredible response, with letters and phone calls coming in every day for months. The communications came from old friends and from people we had never met. It was very exciting to answer the phone and to open our mail every day.

We heard from past district governors of Rotary we had trained with in Nashville, Tennessee; from business associates; from Rotarians who had tracked us down because I mentioned our club, the Rotary Club of The Boundary, in my article.

We heard from old air force friends and from new air force acquaintances. One of the first people to write was Squadron Leader Tony Whitty, Mac's flight commander from 76 Squadron, with whom we had lost touch for over fifty years. We also had a letter from an RAF pilot who now owns a travel agency in California; and as our correspondence with him increased we found that his next-door neighbour is a Norwegian who flew with 76 Squadron. What a small world it is!

A Rotarian who had medical problems similar to Mac's wrote about research in rare diseases. All kinds of interesting letters arrived from California and we also heard from Alberta, Kentucky, New Hampshire, Florida, Vermont, Maine, Ontario, British Columbia and Quebec. We even had a letter in Spanish from Peru. Stanstead College asked to reprint the article in their *Red and White Bulletin*. The Newport Rotary Club invited us to dinner and asked me to speak on the response to the article.

The extraordinary response we received from one small article in the Rotary magazine made us wonder, "Why?" Why did so many people take the trouble to communicate with us, to tell us their stories, to track us down and express their feelings? For example, the doctor who wondered if we might have met his brother, a Canadian flying with the Royal Air Force; the minister who was battling with his conflicting feelings about fighting a war to overcome a great evil but having to kill to do so; the strangers who just wanted to know if there was anything they could do to help.

The most detailed input seemed to be from friends, old and new, who had served with the various air forces and had their memories jogged about those awesome times.

So what kind of people were these flyers who had survived the war, beaten the odds, and over fifty years later rejoiced in making contact? First, they were all volunteers. No one flew as aircrew unless he had made that decision himself. They were brave men, of determination and endurance, patriotic and adventurous. They were young, with young commanding officers, physically fit, intelligent and from a wide variety of social backgrounds. The Royal Air Force, in World War II, was probably the most international force of its size to be found anywhere: Polish, French, Dutch, Rhodesian, Czechoslovakian, Norwegian, Canadian, Australian, New Zealander, and British, to name a few.

Old aviators getting together show a great and well-deserved pride in their service, and that is probably why so many contacts were made after my article was published. Perhaps that is also why so many ex-air force Rotarians are attracted to the international aspects of Rotary.

Sir Arthur Harris said that if he were asked what were the relations between Bomber Command and the American Air Force, he would say that we had no relations—we and they were one force. The Americans gave us the best they had and we did everything possible for them in return. He considered the American bomber crews "the bravest of the brave," remarking that he knew he was speaking for his own bomber crews when he paid this tribute and he had a great deal of admiration for the American commanders.

One of the things we found most interesting, after my article was published, was the contacts with Americans who wrote about their memories of flying with the 8th Air Force. Harry Selling, of California, for example, shared stories by phone and exchanged books and magazines with us. Harry also had some exciting tales of his own adventures from his first operation to the time he was shot down and became a prisoner of war. He was in a camp at Barth in the Baltic, the same prisoner-of-war camp in which Ken Mason was interred.

CHAPTER 26

Strange Encounters

I BELIEVE THE MOST interesting story Mac and I heard after "The Light From Within" was published was that of an encounter between *Oberleutnant* Franz Stigler, a German fighter ace, and Charles Brown, a second lieutenant with the American 379th Bomber Group—a fascinating story of two enemies who became very good friends. Harry Selling asked us if we were familiar with this story, and when we said "no," he sent us all the information together with a very interesting tape.

On December 20, 1943, units of the 8th Bomber Command attacked targets in Bremen, Germany. A B-17 aircraft piloted by Charles Brown was severely damaged by flak on the bomb run, including destruction of the Plexiglas nose and damage to two engines. Shortly thereafter, while flying alone, the B-17 was attacked by fifteen Luftwaffe fighters. The heavy damage was compounded in that only two guns out of eleven were functional in the B-17 because of the extreme cold (-60° C).

Even with the limited defensive firepower, the B-17 shot down one fighter and probably downed a second. During the thirteen-minute engagement the oxygen system of the B-17 was knocked out and the crew became unconscious. Although the exact facts are not known, the Fortress is believed to have spiralled from a height of 25,000 feet to less than 500 feet. This unplanned and normally fatal manoeuvre and miraculous recovery probably explains how the bomber survived the attacks by the vastly superior German fighter force. Although the B-17 remained airborne, it had suffered additional fighter-inflicted damage of a critical nature; one of the crew was dead and four others were casualties, including one with his leg blown off.

Well after the fighter engagement had ended, a single ME-109 made a non-firing approach to the crippled B-17 and ended up, for some unknown reason, flying formation on its right wing. The German pilot of the ME-109 nodded to the B-17 pilot, inspected the

American aircraft, and ended up escorting it between some islands in the North Sea. At this point, when the B-17 pilot turned to try to make the difficult trip back to England, the German pilot saluted him and departed. The pilot of the B-17 and his crew were puzzled but assumed that the German had run out of ammunition and that was what had saved them from further attacks.

With some of the crew too severely hurt to attempt a bailout over northern Germany, the rest of the crew had previously decided to stay with the crippled aircraft and to try and make it back home. With so much severe damage, even after throwing out all of the movable equipment, the B-17 could barely limp back to England; but they managed, with great skill and luck, to arrive back at a 250-foot altitude and complete an emergency landing at Seething, a base very near the coast.

Charles Brown and his remaining crew often thought about the German pilot who had not attacked them, and over the years they wondered many times if he had, indeed, run out of ammunition; and if not, why he had not opened fire on them. More than forty years after the event, Charles Brown, the American pilot, initiated an extensive search in an attempt to locate the German pilot.

Eventually, in December 1989, after many failed attempts at contact, a letter written by Brown was published in *Jagerblatt*, a newsletter for former Luftwaffe and current German Air Force fighter pilots, asking for information.

On January 10, 1990, K. Franz Stigler, former *Oberleutnant*, No. 6 JG-27 Luftwaffe Fighter Force, World War II, responded—from his home in Surrey, British Columbia, Canada!

After considerable correspondence, phone calls, and discussion of details, it was confirmed that Stigler was the pilot of the lone ME-109 that did not attempt to finish off the helpless B-17 and crew. Franz Stigler's rare and compassionate act of valour was, at that time, a court martial offence for which he could have been tried and, under extreme sentence, executed.

In describing his actions he explained that as he approached the rear of the disabled bomber he noticed that the tail gunner was slumped over his guns. As he pulled alongside the badly damaged aircraft he could hardly believe what he saw. The B-17 was like a sieve and there was blood everywhere.

"I could see that the crew was having a terrible time dealing with their wounded and struggling to stay in the air," he said. "I was amazed the aircraft could still fly. I thought to myself, 'How can I shoot something like that? I cannot kill these half-dead people.' I saw badly wounded and defenceless men on board rather than just the airplane which was our normal target. It was one thing to shoot at an airplane but in this case I saw the men. I just could not do it."

He described the badly crippled bomber as being "the most severely damaged airplane that he ever saw which was still flying."

Then, in one of those rare moments of compassion in a brutal war, Franz Stigler did an extraordinary thing. He saluted, rolled his fighter, and departed.

When the two pilots finally met they learned a great deal about each other, such as the fact that when they made that fateful encounter, Brown was a young American flying his first operational mission and Stigler was a German fighter ace with twenty-eight confirmed victories against the Western Allies.

It was determined that Stigler's aircraft was fully armed at this time.

At the 179th Bomb Group Association Reunion in October 1990, the ex-Luftwaffe fighter ace and his wife were guests of the association and Stigler was recognized for exceptional compassion and chivalry during the 1943 encounter.

The two pilots became good friends, visiting each other in their respective homes and enjoying each other's company. And the story was told over and over of the time when the B-17, named *Ye Old Pub*, was allowed to struggle home to its English base.

CHAPTER 27

Remember When

WHEN I STARTED THIS BOOK, my ambition was to have it completed by my eightieth birthday. So far I am on target.

Writing *Our Mornings May Never Be* has been an incredible experience. The flashbacks to both horrendous and wonderful times; the contact with friends, old and new; the discovery of previously unknown information; the depth of bitterness felt by Mac and me and by many air force personnel when some of today's armchair historians present their revisionist history.

When we look back on those times with 76 Squadron, we think of the boys from many nations who flew together, fought together, and all too often died together, in the cause of freedom.

Mac and I have always felt grateful that we were able to be on the same base as he flew his operations and that I could know, as quickly as possible, that he had returned from each mission and lived to fight another day. It was a time of sharing our lives that will always be with us.

When Sir Arthur Harris spoke of the extraordinary devotion and heroism of the wartime crews, he said that they saved England from being a mere appanage of Hitler's 1,000-year Reich. Mac and I believe it is very important that our children's and our grandchildren's generations fully understand how much they owe to people such as the aircrews of 76 Squadron for the fact that they are free and not enslaved by a so-called "master race."

* * *

On our fiftieth wedding anniversary, our children took us to The Balsams in New Hampshire for a fabulous weekend. One of the special things they did was to present us with a *Remember When* book with photographs and messages from family and friends.

Of all the contributions in the book we think perhaps the most poignant remarks were made by the youngest contributor, our sixteen-year-old grandson, who wrote: "You have shared your love and knowledge with me as I have grown. From everything you have given me, that is what I will remember most."

What Mac and I remember most, from those long-ago days, are the more than fifty percent of our friends and fellow flyers who never came back, who never had a chance to delight in their children and grandchildren—whose mornings never were.

> "They shall not grow old, as we that are left grow old,
> Age shall not weary them, nor the years condemn.
> At the going down of the sun and in the morning
> We will remember them."

Celebration at The Balsams. L to R: Joan and Mac; Katie; Derek   JOAN MACDONALD

Our family. Top left, Joan and Mac; top right, Lise and John; bottom left: Keith, Joan and Mac; bottom right: Heather and John   *JOAN MACDONALD*

APPENDIX A

Order of the Day posted on HQ Notice Board at RAF Holme on Spalding Moor.

Serial No. 52. May 10, 1945.

COMMAND ROUTINE ORDERS BY

AIR CHIEF MARSHAL SIR A.T. HARRIS, KCB, OBE, AFC.

A 52. PART 1. ADMINISTRATIVE.

SPECIAL ORDER OF THE DAY

Men and Women of Bomber Command.

More than 5 1/2 years ago, within hours of the declaration of War, Bomber Command first assailed the German enemy.

You were then but a handful. Inadequate in everything but the skill and determination of the crews for that sombre occasion and for the unknown years of unceasing battle which lay beyond horizons black indeed.

You, the aircrews of Bomber Command, sent your first ton of bombs away on the morrow of the outbreak of war. A million tons of bombs and mines have followed from Bomber Command alone. From Declaration of War to Cease Fire a continuity of battle without precedent and without relent.

In the Battle of France your every endeavour bore down upon an overwhelming and triumphant enemy.

After Dunkirk, your Country stood alone—in arms but largely unarmed—between the Nazi tyranny and domination of the world.

The Battle of Britain, in which you took great part, raised the last barrier strained but holding in the path of the all-conquering Wehrmacht and the bomb smoke of the Channel ports choked back down German throats the very word "Invasion": not again to find expression within those narrow seas until the bomb-disrupted defences of the Normandy beachheads fell to our combined assault.

In the long years between much was to pass.

Then it was that you, and you for long alone, carried the war ever deeper and ever more furiously into the heart of the Third Reich. There the whole might of the German enemy in undivided strength, and—scarcely less a foe—the very elements, arrayed against you. You overcame them both.

Through those desperate years, undismayed by any odds, undeterred by any casualties, night succeeding night, you fought. The Phalanx of the United Nations.

You fought alone, as the one force then assailing German soil, you fought alone as individuals—isolated in your crew stations by the darkness and the murk, and from all other aircraft in company.

Not for you the hot emulation of high endeavour in the glare and panoply of martial array. Each crew, each one in each crew, fought alone through black nights rent only, mile after continuing mile, by the fiercest barrages ever raised and the instant sally of the searchlights. In each dark minute of those long miles lurked menace. Fog, ice, snow and tempest found you undeterred.

In that loneliness in action lay the final test, the ultimate stretch of human staunchness and determination.

Your losses mounted through those years. Years in which your chance of survival through one spell of operational duty was negligible. Through two periods, mathematically Nil. Nevertheless survivors pressed forward as volunteers to pit their desperately acquired skill in even a third period of operations, on special tasks.

In those 5 years and 3 months of continuous battle over enemy soil, your casualties over long periods were grievous. As the count is cleared those of Bomber Command who gave their lives to bring near to impotence an enemy who had surged swift in triumph through a Continent, and to enable the United Nations to deploy in full array, will be found not less than the total dead of our National Invasion Armies now in Germany.

In the whole history of our National Forces never have so small a band of men been called to support so long such odds. You indeed bore the brunt.

To you who survive I would say this. Content yourselves and take credit with those who perished, that now the "Cease Fire" has sounded, countless homes within our Empire will welcome back a father or a son whose life, but for your endeavours and your sacrifices, would assuredly have been expended during long further years of agony to achieve a victory already ours. No Allied Nation is clear of this debt to you.

I cannot here expound your full achievements.

Your attacks on the industrial centres of Northern Italy did much toward the collapse of the Italian and German Armies in North Africa, and to further invasion of the Italian mainland.

Of the German enemy two to three million fit men, potentially vast armies, were continuously held throughout the war in direct and indirect defence against your assaults. A great part of her industrial war effort went towards fending off your attacks.

You struck a critical proportion of the weapons of war from enemy hands, on every front.

You immobilised armies, leaving them shorn of supplies, reinforcements, resources and reserves, the easier prey to our advancing Forces.

You eased and abetted the passage of our troops over major obstacles. You blasted the enemy from long prepared defences where he essayed to hold. On the Normandy beaches. At the hinge of the Battle of Caen. In the jaws of the Falaise Gap. To the strongpoints of the enemy-held Channel ports, St. Vith, Houffalize and the passage of the Rhine. In battle after battle you sped our armies to success at minimum cost to our troops. The Commanders of our land forces, and indeed those of the enemy, have called your attacks decisive.

You enormously disrupted every enemy means of communication, the very life-blood of his military and economic machines, railways, canals and every form of transport fell first to decay and then to chaos under your assaults.

You so shattered the enemy's oil plants as to deprive him of all but the final trickle of fuel. His aircraft became earthbound, his road transport ceased to roll, armoured fighting vehicles lay helpless outside the battle, or fell immobilised into our hands. His strategic and tactical plans failed through inability to move.

From his war industries supplies of ore, coal, steel, fine metals, aircraft, guns, ammunition, tanks, vehicles and every ancillary equipment dwindled under your attacks.

At the very crisis of the invasion of Normandy, you virtually annihilated the German naval surface forces then in the Channel, a hundred craft and more fell victim to those three attacks.

You sank or damaged a large but yet untotalled number of enemy submarines in his ports and by mine-laying in his waters.

You interfered widely and repeatedly with his submarine training programmes.

With extraordinary accuracy, regardless of opposition, you hit and burst through every carapace which he could devise to protect his submarines in harbour.

By your attacks on inland industries and coastal shipyards you caused hundreds of his submarines to be stillborn.

Your mine laying throughout the enemy's sea lanes, your bombing of his inland waters, and his Ports, confounded his sea traffic, and burst his canals. From Norway throughout the Baltic, from Jutland to the Girondo, on the coasts of Italy and North Africa you laid and re-laid the minefields. The wreckage of the enemy's naval and merchant fleets litters and encumbers his sea lanes and dockyards. A thousand known ships, and many more as yet unknown, fell casualty to your mines.

You hunted and harried his major warships from hide to hide. You put out of action, gutted or sank most of them.

By your attacks on Experimental Stations, factories, communications and firing sites you long postponed and much reduced the V-weapon attacks. You averted an enormous further toll of death and destruction from your Country.

With it all you never ceased to rot the very heart out of the enemy's war resources and resistance.

His Capital and near 100 of his cities and towns including nearly all of leading war industrial importance lie in utter ruin, together with the greater part of the war industry which they supported.

Thus you brought to naught the enemy's original advantage of an industrial might intrinsically greater than ours and supported by the labour of captive millions, now set free.

For the first time in more than a century you have brought home to the habitual aggressor of Europe the full and acrid flavours of war, so long the perquisite of his victims.

All this, and much more, have you achieved during those $5\frac{1}{2}$ years of continuous battle, despite all opposition from an enemy disposing of many a geographical and strategical advantage with which to exploit an initial superiority in numbers.

Men from every part of the Empire and most of the Allied Nations fought in our ranks. Indeed a band of brothers.

In the third year of war the Eighth Bomber Command and the Fifteenth Bomber Command, USAAF from their Mediterranean bases, ranged themselves at our side, zealous in extending even mutual aid, vying in every assault upon our common foe. Especially they played the leading part in sweeping the enemy fighter definitely from our path, and, finally, out of the skies.

Nevertheless nothing that the crews accomplished—[which] was much, and decisive—could have been achieved without the devoted service of every man and woman in the Command.

Those who tendered the aircraft, mostly in the open, through six bitter winters. Endless intricacies in a prolonged misery of wet and cold. They rightly earned the implicit trust of the crews. They set extraordinary records of aircraft serviceability.

Those who manned the Stations, Operational Headquarters, Supply lines and Communications.

The pilots of the Photographic Reconnaissance Units without whose lonely ventures far and wide over enemy territory we should have been largely powerless to plan or to strike.

The Operational Crew training organisation of the Command which through these years of ceaseless work by day and night never failed, in the face of every difficulty and unproductive call, to replace all casualties and to keep our constantly expanding first line up to strength in crews trained to the highest pitch of efficiency; simultaneously producing near 20,000 additional trained aircrew for the raising and reinforcement of some 50 extra squadrons, formed in the Command and despatched for service in other Commands at home and overseas.

The men and women of the Meteorological Branch who attained prodigious exactitudes in a fickle art and stood brave on assertion where science is inexact. Time and again they saved us from worse than the enemy could ever have achieved. Their record is outstanding.

The meteorological reconnaissance pilots, who flew through anything and everything in search of the feasible.

The Operational Research Sections whose meticulous investigation of every detail of every attack provided data for the continuous confounding of the enemy and the consistent reduction of our own casualties.

The scientists, especially those of the Telecommunications Research Establishment, who placed in unending succession in our hands, the technical means to resolve our problems and to confuse the every parry of the enemy. Without their skill and their labours beyond doubt we could not have prevailed.

The Works Services who engineered for Bomber Command alone 2,000 miles of runway, track and road, with all that goes with them.

The Works Staffs, Designers and Workers who equipped and re-equipped us for Battle. Their efforts, their honest workmanship, kept in our hands indeed a Shining Sword.

To all of you I would say how proud I am to have served in Bomber Command for 4^1/2 years and to have been your Commander-in-Chief through more than three years of your Saga.

Your task in the German war is now completed. Famously have you fought. Well have you deserved of your country and her Allies.

(Signed) AT HARRIS

Air Chief Marshal
Commander-in-Chief

BOMBER COMMAND

APPENDIX B

AS WE REMEMBER THEM

One of the most famous bomber pilots of World War II, Lord Cheshire (Group Captain, VC, DSO and two bars, DFC, Order of Merit—1981, Life Peer), was commanding officer of 76 Squadron from August 1942 to April 1943. He was a much-admired pilot who not only completed three tours of operations—an almost unheard-of feat—but also acted as his own test pilot. He discovered faults that were common in the Halifaxes at that time and struggled to get them corrected—in some cases taking the initiative and correcting them himself.

He pleaded for design changes in the tail section because of lack of control that led to crashes, and proved his point by putting the bomber into a spin, only just recovering in time.

On the lighter side, he took the time to know as many of the people on the station as possible and he earned their admiration by caring enough to do things such as taking a tray of goodies to the WAAF on night duty when they were missing a party!

When Cheshire was posted to Marston Moor and he handed over the Squadron to Wing Commander Don Smith, the Squadron diarist wrote: "What the Squadron has lost, Marston Moor will gain. It was under the character and personal supervision of Group Captain Cheshire that the Squadron became what it is today, one of the best in Bomber Command."

However, upon his promotion to group captain and his command of Marston Moor, where the aircrews were converting to Halifaxes, Cheshire was not happy with his assignment. He said he felt too young and inexperienced in administration to be a station commander, and he tried very hard to get back on operations again.

To do this, he had to revert back to wing commander, and he was then given command of 617 Squadron, the famous squadron that had been formed earlier to blow up the Mohne and Eder dams in the Ruhr. His task now was to devise a method of destroying Hitler's most menacing secret weapon of all, the V3, which, when ready, would be able to pump a 200-pound bomb into London every two minutes.

His squadron volunteers, all of whom had excelled on their previous tours, made forty attacks against military targets in France, preparing techniques for hitting the gun silos while inflicting virtually no civilian casualties.

Cheshire was awarded the Victoria Cross on completing one hundred bombing missions over Europe.

He witnessed the use of the atomic bomb against Japan.

After the war was over, Cheshire dedicated his life to those who were sick, disabled or disadvantaged, and was recognized throughout the world for his untiring compassionate work. One hundred-and-eighty-five "Cheshire Homes" spread throughout the world provide full-time residential care for people no longer able to remain in their own homes.

A Holme oak tree with a plaque has been placed in Cheshire's memory at our airfield. On September 25, 1992, there was a memorial service at Westminster Cathedral. At the same time—twelve noon—services were held at every Cheshire Home in the world.

* * *

Group captain Pelly-Fry was posted to Holme on Spalding Moor bomber base in 1944, shortly after completing a year as an equerry to King George VI at Buckingham Palace.

At thirty-two years of age, he was the new station commander. The commanding officer of 76 Squadron at Holme was Wing Commander Hank Iveson, whom Group Captain Pelly-Fry described as "direct, competent and friendly." The two men were obviously compatible, which led to a squadron with high efficiency and morale.

Hank was a colourful character well known in Bomber Command. With his tall stature, flowing moustache, infectious grin and many gongs (medals), he commanded 76 Squadron in a firm, no-nonsense, but friendly way. His courage was legendary and his opinions definite. He proposed to his wife, Margaret, who was a Red Cross nurse, within an hour of meeting her! His son is now also a pilot, also a wing commander, and also named Hank!

Group Captain Douglas 'Hank' Iveson

Iveson (1963);
Bomber

GROUP CAPTAIN Douglas "Hank" Iveson, an heroic Second World War bomber pilot, has died, aged 77.

Hull born Mr Iveson, was training as a structural engineer when war broke out and joined up as a pilot, flying Whitley and Halifax bombers, often from Yorkshire.

He completed two full tours of ops over Germany with No. 77 Squadron based at Topcliffe and Leeming, and with 76 squadron as flight commander at Middleton St George, County Durham.

The pinnacle of his career was commanding 76 squadron from November 1943 to August 1944 at Holme upon Spalding Moor, Humberside, for which he received the Distinguished Service Order.

He also won two Distinguished Flying Crosses, one for circling over a target area to draw off fire from anti aircraft guns while the rest of the squadron attacked the battleship Tirpitz at Trondheim naval base in 1942.

His other DFC was for a daylight raid on Crete and low level attack on gun emplacements while on his third tour, based in North Africa.

He also took part in three 1,000 bomber raids against Cologne, Hamburg, and Essen and ten raids on Tobruk. His aircraft shot down two ME 109 fighters.

Mr Iveson — nicknamed Hank after the cartoon character because of his huge moustache — finished the war as an acting Wing Commander, but was to stay on in the RAF until he was 50.

He flew bombers in the United States, was a staff officer at Bomber Command (now Strike Command) at High Wycombe, and commanded another two squadrons.

He was the chief instructor who taught the first jet bomber crews in the Valiant and Victor aircraft at RAF Gaydon, near Warwick.

It was while there he set the air speed record from Farnborough to Malta on October 1958 in a Victor, averaging 655mph at 35,000ft, in two hours and 43 seconds.

He later went on to command a station of Vulcans himself at RAF Waddington, near Lincoln.

He was then based in Singapore as Chief of Intelligence for the Far East Air Force, ending up at signal command headquarters in Buckinghamshire, from where he retired in 1967.

In civvie street, he became director of the combined Sheffield and Rotherham Chambers of Commerce before retiring to Filey, where he had gone on holiday as a boy.

His son Robert, also a Wing Commander, said yesterday: "He was a larger than life man in all respects. He was 6ft 3½in tall and had size 14 shoes."

He was a devoted, father and family man, who proposed to his wife, Margaret, within an hour of meeting her while she was working as a Red Cross nurse at RAF Brize Norton, near Oxford.

His son said: "He always said as a joke that wartime marriages never last but they were married 53 years, and she died only two months before him. It was love at first sight.

"He was devoted father to myself and my three sisters, and had eight grandchildren who worshipped him."

Mr Iveson died at Scarborough's St Catherine's Hospice. His funeral will take place on Thursday at Filey Methodist Church.

The family have requested donations be sent to St Catherine's or Cancer Research, care of A Haxey and Son, 7 Belle Vue Street, Filey

FROM THE *DAILY TELEGRAPH* – DEC. 29, 94

Group Captain James Pelly-Fry

GROUP CAPTAIN JAMES PELLY-FRY, who has died aged 83, led "Pelly-Fry's Hell Divers" against Italian targets in East Africa in 1940, and two years later was awarded the DSO for his part in Operation Oyster, 2 Group's biggest and most complex air attack of the war.

In December 1942, as commander of 88 Squadron of Douglas Boston light bombers, Pelly-Fry led one of the eight squadrons briefed to destroy the Phillips factory at Eindhoven, which supplied Germany with a third of its electronics products.

A high-level night attack by Bomber Command had been ruled out in order to minimise civilian casualties, and at lunchtime on Dec 6 the force of about 100 light bombers swept low over the Dutch coast.

Despite an escort of three fighter squadrons on the homeward trip, the daylight sortie was a risky enterprise. Flying at 250 mph at "zero feet" left no room for error; the ground rushed past, Pelly-Fry recalled, "in a blur of fields, minor roads, streams and farm buildings"

Flocks of birds on the Dutch mudflats were an additional hazard; the aircrafts' canopies and wings became plastered with blood and feathers.

Although attacked by FW 190 fighters, the force pressed on. As Pelly-Fry directed his Boston at the main factory building he was so low that the German anti-aircraft gunners on the roof were actually firing down at him.

Hit by the flak, he noticed that part of the starboard wing was sticking up vertically and the fabric on one of the ailerons was shredding in the slipstream. Then the starboard engine began an ominous rattle until, throttled back, it quietened.

He then found that there were two FW 190s on his tail.

Pelly-Fry in the 1940s

Only Pelly-Fry's evasive skill and the German pilots' apparent inexperience enabled him to lose them over the North Sea.

Losing height, he managed to make a belly-landing on one engine. Nine Venturas, four Bostons and one Mosquito had been lost in the operation, but the Phillips factory had been effectively demolished. It was six months before it resumed production.

When Pelly-Fry visited the works after the war — at the invitation of the Phillips directors — he was congratulated on the havoc wreaked by the raid.

James Ernest Pelly-Fry was born on Nov 22 1911 and educated at Douai School. After the death of his father, a Ceylon tea expert, he entered the accounts department of the P & O Shipping Company, at the age of 14.

Two years later he was apprenticed to Joseph Tetley & Son. His hobby was aeromodelling; he flew his own designs on Wimbledon Common and became a council member of the recently formed Society of Model Aeronautical Engineers. But he hankered after the real thing.

In 1933 Pelly-Fry was accepted for the Reserve of

Air Force Officers, and the next year he joined an air charter firm at Heston Aerodrome, Middlesex, to fly Fleet Street newspapers to Paris.

The RAF offered him a short-service commission in 1935 and he was posted to 216 Squadron, flying biplane Vickers Valentias in Egypt.

In late 1938 Pelly-Fry was selected as personal assistant to Air Cdre Arthur Harris, then air commander in Palestine. Harris dubbed him "Pelly" and the nickname stuck.

In 1939 he went as flight lieutenant to 223 Squadron, flying Vickers Wellesleys out of Nairobi in Kenya. When Italy entered the war in June 1940 Pelly-Fry was immediately in action, and in August he received command of 47 Squadron, also in the Wellesley wing.

He was next posted as Joint Senior RAF Intelligence Officer Western Desert and, in the spring of 1941, was involved in the relief of RAF Habbanya, under siege from the rebel force of the Iraqi potentate Raschid Ali.

After making a chance recovery of an Me 110 fighter from the Iraqi desert Pelly-Fry was inspired to set up a small RAF version of the Army's Long Range Desert Group to gather intelligence in the Western Desert.

In 1942 he returned to Britain, where he joined 88 Squadron, whose Douglas Boston light bombers had just arrived from the United States. Pelly-Fry took part in operations over France, including the Dieppe raid, and his squadron established a warm relationship with its fighter escorts.

The wing leader would call "Hi-de-hi!" to the fighter pilots, who would respond enthusiastically, "Pelly-Fry!"

When his crews were billeted at Blickling Hall, the Marquess of Lothian's house in East Anglia, Pelly-Fry was

nicknamed "Baron Fry of Blickling".

After a strenuous tour of operations Pelly-Fry was — to his astonishment — appointed Air Equerry to the King in 1943, and moved into Buckingham Palace. Several months later he discreetly arranged to get back to the war.

Now a group captain, Pelly-Fry received command of a Halifax bomber station, RAF Holme-in-Spalding-Moor. In 1945 he was posted to Australia to command RAF Camden, near Sydney.

After demobilisation in 1946 he flew briefly in Kenya as a charter pilot but, disillusioned with civilian life, he returned to the RAF with a permanent commission. He re-entered as a squadron leader, until posted to RAF Syerston as Wing Commander Administration. He was appointed to the RAF Personnel Selection Board, and staff appointments in Nato followed.

In 1955, once more a group captain, he was appointed air attaché in Teheran. His remarkable rapport with leading figures in the Shah of Iran's regime was of great value to Britain, generating substantial export business for the aviation industry.

Pelly-Fry retired from the RAF in 1958, but was engaged by the Commonwealth Office, acting as their civil air attaché for Australia and New Zealand until 1962. He then joined the aircraft manufacturer Handley Page, but the company soon folded.

After training in Harrods' Food Hall Pelly-Fry opened Epicure of Chichester, a delicatessen in Sussex. In the early 1970s he sold the business and moved to Somerset, where he resumed his building of model aeroplanes. He recently published a volume of autobiography, *Heavenly Days*.

He married, in 1949, Mrs Irene Ritchie (née Dunsford), who predeceased him; they had a son.

116

APPENDIX C

Phil Judkins: Toast to "The Squadron" at 2001 Reunion of 76 Squadron

"THE FUNDAMENTAL THINGS APPLY"

In fact it was my father, Ted Judkins, who flew his second tour with 76 from Holme on Spalding Moor. I am, therefore, proposing this toast from the perspective of a different generation. In that generation, there have been many critics of what Bomber Command achieved. Frank Robertson powerfully and rightly dealt with them last year. I can't match Frank's eloquence, but I can reinforce it with some views from my own and later generations.

As 76's archivist, I've read many, many books, as much as I can, on Bomber Command. At the end it's like the song "As Time Goes By"—remember, from the film *Casablanca*? "The Fundamental Things Apply."

What are those Fundamental Things? I think there are five.

First, the British did not want to go to war, but their duty was carried out. About once every twenty-five years or so, it seems, some madman arises—the Kaiser, Hitler, Galtieri, Hussein, Milosevic—and we get involved. Strange nation, the British. We have to sort out some really major problems and we then spend the next twenty-five years arguing and criticising about how we might have done it better. Maybe the Fundamental Thing is that it was done at all—that the fight was made, and won.

Second, when eventually there is no alternative to war, you fight to win.

Churchill put it best; he said, "You ask, what are our war aims? I answer in one word, victory." Many critics say, "but we should not have prevailed so strongly": what an odd thing to say, when we were opposing the blackest tyranny ever! Perhaps the strangest compliment of all comes from Dr. Josef Goebbels; advising his family in 1945 in a Berlin bunker, he said, "Head for the British lines; when the world falls to pieces the British will act properly."

Third, what other means of attack had we then, if not bombing? After Dunkirk, we had only an army with no equipment. What were we supposed to do? Shout "Yah boo"? Give up? I doubt it.

Fourth, there has been a lot of criticism of the extent of the damage. People seem horrified at any damage now; but isn't it easy for a later age, with satellite navigation able to plant bombs within a metre, to criticise? With the tools and techniques of sixty years ago, it was impossible to be any more accurate: if our radar group had been able to be here, they would have told you, you were pushing well beyond the limits even then. The Fundamental Thing—it was impossible to be any more accurate.

Fifth, the awesome scale of sacrifice commands respect. The World War I trenches are rightly a horror; factually, more bomber crewmen died in 1939–1945 than infantry officers in the trenches in 1914–18. The scale of the loss in bombers was unparalleled—sixty from every 100 aircrew died (fifty-one on operations, nine in training in the UK), three from every 100 were injured, twelve prisoners of war, one evaded, and twenty-four survived. Of the 76 family, as Bill Chorley has well recorded, 780 died or died of wounds.

The consequence—peace for nearly sixty years; maybe uneasy peace, but peace for your children—my generation—and your grandchildren—my children—to grow up in.

In case no one else says it, THANK YOU, from their generation and mine.

The sacrifice of 76, and the peace it achieved: Those Fundamental Things Apply.

76's duty was carried out, and Resolutely.

Therefore I ask you to be upstanding and raise your glasses with me, to "76 SQUADRON!"

(September 8, 2001)

APPENDIX D

THE 76 SQUADRON MEMORIAL WINDOW

Prominently displayed in the right-hand light of the window is the Squadron badge, with the motto "Resolute," a very fitting word for the aircrews of 76 Squadron as they departed on their missions, and one that became a part of all our lives. Below the Squadron badge are three anchors, a reminder of the losses suffered by the Squadron during action against three German battleships, the *Scharnhorst*, *Gneisenau* and *Tirpitz*. Our own group captain, Hank Iveson, was awarded one of his two Distinguished Flying Crosses for circling over a target area to draw off fire from anti-aircraft guns while the rest of the Squadron attacked the battleship *Tirpitz* at Trondheim Naval Base in 1942.

All Saints Church itself is depicted on the left-hand light with the red beacon shining from the tower against a lightening sky in which is a handful of stars. The ancient parish church seems to blend beautifully with the more modern interpretation of the stars.

The main central area of the design is composed of two large interlocked circles; the upper edge of the lower circle is marked for a compass rose, and the central area represents the landscape of Yorkshire, in which the church and the airfield of Holme on Spalding Moor are situated.

The Hercules radial engine, shown at the base of the right-hand light, will bring back many memories to 76 Squadron pilots.

The words "To See the Dawn Breaking—Safely Holme" describes the crews as they make it back over the English coast, cold and exhausted, with another operation almost completed toward their tour of duty and, hopefully, their eventual screening. Also, W.R. Chorley, who wrote the history of 76 Squadron, entitled his book *To See the Dawn Breaking*.

The yellow lines in the lower half of each light depict the runways of the airfield. We remembered those wide runways and visualized the lumbering Halifaxes with their heavy bomb loads taking off and disappearing into the distance on their dangerous missions; and we thought, as always, of the crews who did not return—who would never again see the dawn breaking.

Probably for most of us the most personal and memorable part of the images and symbols was at the top of the right-hand light where two Halifax bombers are returning from ops, guided in over the early morning fields by the red beacon; on the left-hand light are the upturned faces of two ground crew who are eagerly awaiting their return.

Two quotations complete the window. One, a simple "In Memory of 76 Squadron, RAF"; and the other, some verses by Minnie Louise Haskins (1873–1957). The text is an extract from "God Knows," and reads:

And I said to the man who stood at the gate of the year;

'Give me a light that I may tread safely into the unknown'

And he replied:

'Go out into the darkness and put your hand into the hand of God.

That shall be to you better than light and safer than a known way.'

* * *

The following instructions may help returning veterans and their families who would like to see this window.

The Parish Church of All Saints is east of Holme on Spalding Moor Village and about twenty-six miles from the city of York. Take the 1079, which is the main road from York to Hull. The road will be side-posted to Holme on Spalding Moor.

The church is kept locked when not attended, but the vicar would be happy to show you the *Book of Remembrance* and the stained glass window donated by the 76 Squadron Organization. You can contact him at the vicarage or call him at 0430 860248.

Returning Squadron personnel might like to have lunch at one of their old haunts in the village; Ye Old Red Lion and The Cross Keys Pub are still going strong.

They can also visit their old airfield at Skiff Lane. Some of the buildings, such as the officers' mess, are still standing.

Just past the guardhouse is a site with memorials to 76 Squadron and to 458 Squadron of the Royal Australian Air Force, who were at Holme before 76 Squadron arrived. Trees have been planted and plaques displayed in memory of Group Captain Lord Cheshire, VC, OM, DSO, DFC; and

Group Captain Douglas "Hank" Iveson, DSO, DFC, both commanding officers of 76 Squadron.

The oak seat presented by John Coward and crafted by George Woods enables the visitor to rest and remember.

Memorial for 76 Squadron   JOAN MACDONALD

APPENDIX E

LEAFLETS DROPPED FOR THE INFORMATION OF THE GERMAN POPULATION

One method of contacting the Germans was to drop leaflets (known as "nickels") from our aircraft.

The following three leaflets were such messages to the German people from General Dwight D. Eisenhower, Supreme Commander of the Allied Fighting Forces.

LEAFLET #1: SIDE 1

THE CHOICE

Photo of Himmler	Photo of Eisenhower

Reichsfuehrer Heinrich Himmler	**General Dwight D. Eisenhower**
Supreme commander of the National Army, *Reichsfuehrer* of the SS	Supreme commander of the Allied Fighting Forces.

HIMMLER	*EISENHOWER*
Forced displacements, prolonging the war.	Self-protection by the people against the SS, shortening the war.
Bombs, hunger and SS terror on the battlefield, Germany.	Safety, order and air protection under the Anglo-American military government.

All orders and directions from the Supreme Commander of the Allied Fighting Forces, General Dwight D. Eisenhower, are broadcast in German by Radio Luxemburg and London

DIE WAHL

REICHSFÜHRER HEINRICH HIMMLER

Oberbefehlshaber des Heimatheeres, Reichsführer SS

GENERAL DWIGHT D. EISENHOWER

Oberbefehlshaber der Alliierten Streitkräfte

HIMMLER

Zwangsverschleppung zur Verlängerung des Krieges.

Bomben, Hunger und SS-Terror auf dem Schlachtfeld Deutschland.

EISENHOWER

Volks-Selbstschutz gegen SS zur Verkürzung des Krieges.

Sicherheit, Ordnung und Luftschutz unter anglo-amerikanischer Militär-Regierung.

Alle Verordnungen und Anweisungen des Oberbefehlshabers der Alliierten Streitkräfte, General Dwight D. Eisenhower, werden in deutscher Sprache von den Sendern Radio Luxemburg und London durchgegeben.

W.G.23

LEAFLET #1, SIDE 2

THE AACHEN DISTRICT DEFENDS ITSELF . . .

The decision of the Nazis, desirous of prolonging the war, to move, by force if necessary, the civilian population off to the interior of the Reich, was carried out with indescribable brutality. Everywhere the SS- and SA-bandits used the evacuation order as a pretext to terrorize and plunder the population. Nevertheless, in almost all cities and villages of the currently occupied areas thousands of families were able to save themselves, and successfully offer resistance against the party terror.

TODAY THE FACTS ARE KNOWN:

In Aachen the SS regularly hunted down civilians who refused to give up their house and farm to an unknown fate, and be separated from their families, perhaps never to see them again. It is true that the battle in Aachen, ordered by Hitler, brought about the destruction of the city. However, thousands of Aachen families who remained behind are safe today, and in possession of the remainder of their property.

In Kohlscheide the SS commandos carrying out the forced evacuation regularly waged war against the population. Women and mothers were dragged by force into the evacuation trucks and taken away, while the children were left behind in the cellars. Despite this a large proportion of the population was able to hide and get to safety. For them the war is over today.

In KORNELIMUENSTER, BRAND, ESINGEN, GROTENRATH, UBACH and many other communities it was the same picture: Forced evacuation ordered by the party; flight of the party bigwigs; terror and extreme brutality by the SS and SA against the civilian population . . . innumerable acts of robbery, theft and plunder by the SS and SA in houses evacuated by force. Successful SELF PROTECTION of all civilians who actively resisted the order to evacuate.

WHAT IS THE LESSON?

The experiences in Aachen and the villages in the Aachen district prove that resistance against the party terror is possible and successful. Even in the small communities of the Aachen district the will of the population was triumphant over the organized displacement terror by the Party and the SS.

In COLOGNE, DUESSELDORF, DORTMUND and all the large cities under threat of forced evacuation of the Rhine and Ruhr areas, the civilian population can and must OBSTRUCT THE FORCED DISPLACEMENT, AND SAVE THEMSELVES by means of:

MASS RESISTANCE

KREIS AACHEN WEHRT SICH . . .

Der Beschluss der nationalsozialistischen Kriegsverlängerer, die Zivilbevölkerung — wenn nötig mit Gewalt — ins Reichsinnere zu verschleppen,
wurde mit unbeschreiblicher Brutalität durchgeführt. Überall benutzten
die SS- und SA-Banditen den Verschleppungsbefehl als Vorwand, die Bevölkerung zu terrorisieren und auszuplündern. Jedoch in fast allen Städten
und Ortschaften der jetzt besetzten Gebiete konnten sich tausende von
Familien retten und gegen den Parteiterror erfolgreich Widerstand leisten.

HEUTE SIND DIE TATSACHEN BEKANNT:

In Aachen machte die SS regelrechte Jagd auf Zivilisten, die sich
weigerten, Haus und Hof einem unbekannten Schicksal zu
überlassen und sich vielleicht auf Nimmerwiedersehen von
ihren Familien zu trennen. Es ist wahr: die von Hitler befohlene
Schlacht um AACHEN brachte die Vernichtung der Stadt —
aber tausende von zurückgebliebenen Aachener Familien sind
heute in Sicherheit und im Besitze der Reste ihrer Habe.

In Kohlscheide führten die Zwangsräumungs-Kommandos der
SS regulären Krieg gegen die Bevölkerung. Frauen und Mütter
hat man mit Gewalt in die Räumungs-Lastwagen gezerrt und
verschleppt, während die Kinder in den Kellern zurückblieben.
Trotzdem konnte sich ein Grossteil der Bevölkerung verbergen
und in Sicherheit bringen. Für sie ist der Krieg heute vorbei.

In KORNELIMÜNSTER, BRAND, ESINGEN, GROTENRATH,
UBACH und vielen anderen Gemeinden gab es das gleiche Bild:

Zwangsräumungsbefehl der Partei; Flucht der Parteibonzen;
Terror und äusserste Brutalität von SS und SA gegen die
Zivilbevölkerung . . . Zahllose Akte von Raub, Diebstahl und
Plünderung durch SS und SA in den zwangsgeräumten Häusern.
Erfolgreicher SELBSTSCHUTZ aller Zivilisten, die sich
dem Räumungsbefehl aktiv widersetzten.

WAS IST DIE LEHRE ?

Die Erfahrungen von AACHEN und den Ortschaften des
Aachener Gebiets beweisen, dass Widerstand gegen den Partei-
Terror möglich und erfolgreich ist. Selbst in den kleinen
Gemeinden des Aachener Gebiets siegte der Wille der Be-
völkerung über den organisierten Verschleppungsterror von
Partei und SS.

In KÖLN, DÜSSELDORF, DORTMUND und allen von der
Zwangsräumung bedrohten Grosstädten von Rhein und Ruhr
kann und muss die Zivilbevölkerung die ZWANGSVER-
SCHLEPPUNG VERHINDERN UND SICH SELBER RETTEN
durch:

MASSENWIDERSTAND

LEAFLET #2, SIDE 1

THE POST-WAR PERIOD

will be difficult—how difficult depends on you!

In the occupied areas of West Germany the war is over. The SS and Gestapo's terror regime has disappeared. Positions that have been purged of Nazis will gradually be taken over by responsible Germans. The bombing war is over, life goes on—not an easy life, for there is much to do: the next thing will be to clear away the rubble and ruins that were caused by bombs and futile resistance. Gradually, and after hard work, normal circumstances will be reestablished. Self-help will put community life back in full swing—today in the occupied west territory, tomorrow in all Germany.

Self-help means:

YOU bear the cost, when fanatics want to blow up gas, water, and electric works. That will not hold up the Allies, but it will mean more misery for YOU in the coming winter, and greater difficulties in rebuilding YOUR country!

YOUR family will need to scrimp, if fanatics want to remove a steady food supply. The Allied armies bring their own provisions. When food is imported preference will necessarily be given to those areas that are currently suffering hunger due to the German occupation.

Self-help is the order of the hour

- Self-help today—to rescue YOUR family
- Self-help later—to rebuild YOUR homeland

Joan MacDonald

DIE NACHKRIEGSZEI

wird schwer sein — wie schwe
hängt von Dir selbst ab!

In den besetzten Gebieten Westdeutschlands ist der Kri(
vorbei. Das Terror-Regime der SS und Gestapo ist ve
schwunden. Die von Nationalsozialisten gesäuberten Stell(
werden allmählich von verantwortungsvollen Deutsch(
übernommen. Der Bombenkrieg ist vorüber, das Leb(
geht weiter — es ist kein leichtes Leben, denn es gibt viel :
tun: Zunächst werden Schutt und Trümmer, die dur(
Bomben und nutzlosen Widerstand verursacht worden ware
aus dem Weg geschafft. Allmählich und nach schwer
Arbeit werden normale Verhältnisse wiederhergestellt: Selbs
hilfe bringt das Gemeinschaftsleben wieder in Schwung-
heute im besetzten Westgebiet, morgen in ganz Deutschlan(
S e l b s t h i l f e — d a s h e i s s t :

Es geht auf DEINE Kosten, wenn Fanatiker die Gas
Wasser- und Elektrizitätswerke in die Luft sprenge
wollen. Das hält die Alliierten nicht auf. Aber es bedeut(
mehr Elend für DICH im kommenden Winter und grösse(
Schwierigkeiten für den Wiederaufbau DEINES Lande

DEINE Familie wird kargen müssen, wenn Fanatiker di
Lebensmittelbestände fortschleppen wollen. Die alliierte
Heere bringen ihre eigene Verpflegung. Bei der Leben(
mitteleinfuhr werden unbedingten Vorzug aber die Länd(
haben, die auf Grund der deutschen Besetzung jet:
Hunger leiden.

Selbsthilfe ist das Gebot der Stunde

- Selbsthilfe heute — zur Rettung DEINER Famili
- Selbsthilfe später — zum Wiederaufbau DEINER Heim(

WG :

LEAFLET #2, SIDE 2

After the arrival of the Allies

in German territory, military rule was proclaimed through General Dwight D. Eisenhower in his capacity as military governor. Military rule proceeds strictly but justly in the occupied areas. Its chief task is neither to punish nor to educate Germany, but to ensure Allied connections, and to bring about peace as soon as possible. Towards this goal they must remove the Nazi leadership hierarchy as well as apprehend and pass judgment on war criminals. The civilian population will be given the opportunity to go about their daily activities and through self-help once more bring their home areas back into full swing.

[Photo of Eisenhower]

General Dwight D. Eisenhower, supreme commander of the Allied Fighting Forces and military governor.

Photo of American officers and German civilians

American officers from the military government explaining to German civilians the terms of management in an evacuation camp.

NACH DEM EINMARSCH DER ALLIIERTEN

auf deutsches Gebiet erfolgte die Proklamierung der Militärregierung durch General Dwight D. Eisenhower in seiner Eigenschaft als Militär-Gouverneur. Die Militärregierung geht streng aber gerecht in den besetzten Gebieten vor. Ihre Hauptaufgabe ist weder die Bestrafung noch die Erziehung Deutschlands, sondern die Sicherung de~ alliierten Verbindungen, die baldmögliche Herbeiführung des Friedens und zu diesem Zweck die Entfernung der nationalsozialistischen Führerschicht sowie die Festnahme und Aburteilung der Kriegsverbrecher. Der Zivilbevölkerung wird Gelegenheit gegeben, ihren täglichen Beschäf-tigungen nachzugehen und durch Selbsthilfe ihre Heimatorte wieder in Schwung zu bringen.

General Dwight D. Eisenhower
Oberbefehlshaber der alliierten ·Streit-kräfte und Militär-Gouverneur.

Amerikanische Offiziere der Militär-regierung erklären deutschen Zivilisten die Bestimmungen über den Betrieb in einem Evakuierungs-Lager.

LEAFLET #3

German Woman—You Have the Floor!

This is the sixth year of war. The German soldier has returned home. He has endured inhuman sufferings in the killing fields of Russia, in the deserts of Africa, under heavy Allied fire in Italy, and the hail of bombs on the Western Front. Now, once again, he is to take up the fight against the enormous superior force of the Anglo-American war machine—without adequate armored equipment or air force. You, German woman, have the power to avert endless grief, terror and death. To the returned German soldier, say this:

- That you do not want this senseless final resistance.

- That you do not want your towns and villages to be shot to pieces.

- That you have had enough of the SS and the Party, who order destruction of your homeland just so they can remain in power for another few days.

- That in this regard a soldier's loyalty belongs exclusively to the People.

- That the People demand this.

End the war!

Out with those prolonging it!

Deutsche Frau, Du hast das Wort!

Das ist das sechste Kriegsjahr. Der deutsche Soldat ist zurückgekehrt. Er hat Unmenschliches erduldet auf den Schlachtfeldern Russlands, den Wüsten Afrikas, unter dem Trommelfeuer der Alliierten in Italien und dem Bombenhagel an der Westfront. Aufs neue, auf Heimatboden, soll er nun den Kampf gegen die ungeheure Übermacht der anglo-amerikanischen. Kriegsmaschine aufnehmen. Ohne genügend Panzer and Luftwaffe. Du, deutsche Frau, hast die Macht, unendliches Leid, Schrecken und Tod zu verhüten. Sage dem heimgekehrten deutschen Soldaten:

- *Dass Du diesen sinnlosen letzten Widerstand nicht willst.*

- *Dass Du nicht willst, dass Deine Städte and Dôrfer in Grund und Boden geschossen werden.*

- *Dass Du genug hast von der SS und der Partei, die die Zerstörungider Heimat befehlen, nur um sich seiber noch ein paar Tage länger im Sattel zu halten.*

- *Dass Darum Soldatentreue ausschiesslich dem Volke géhört.*

- *Dass dieses Volk verlangt:*

Schluss mit dem Krie!

Weg mit den Kriegsverlängerern!

BIBLIOGRAPHY

Aircrew Association. *Aircrew Memories*. Victoria, BC: The Victoria Publishing Co. Ltd., 1999.

Air Ministry Directorate of Public Relations. *The WAAF in Action*. London: Adam & Charles Black, 1944.

Bomber Command Association. *The Means of Victory*. London: Charterhouse publications Ltd., 1992.

Catchpole, B. *Balloons to Buccaneers*. York: Maxiprint, 1994.

Chorley, W.R. *To See the Dawn Breaking*. Devon: Midland Counties Publications, 1981.

Churchill, W.S. *The Second World War: The Grand Alliance*. Boston: Houghton Mifflin, 1950.

The Halifax Aircraft Association. *Newsletter*. Willowdale, ON: Halifax Aircraft Association, 1995–1999.

Harris, Sir A. *Bomber Offensive*. London: Collins, 1947.

Headrick, R. *A Mighty Fortress*. Dayton, NV: TBD Services Inc., 1992.

Mendi, H. *25 Years of Winston Churchill: Memoirs and Speeches*. England: Polygamy Record Operations, 1994, compact disc.

Miller, A.D. *The White Cliffs*. London: Methuen & Co., 1941.

Morris, R. *Guy Gibson*. London: Penguin Books, 1995.

Palm Springs Air Museum Volunteers. *Voices of World War II*. Europe Edition. Palm Springs, compact disc.

Pelly-Fry, J. *Heavenly Days*. England: Crecy Books, 1994.

Pilkington, G. *Time Remembered*. Burnstown, ON: General Store Publishing House, 1994.

Price, D. & Walley, D. *Never Give In: The Challenging Words of Winston Churchill*. Kansas City, Missouri: Hallmark, 1967.

Seventy-Six Squadron Association. *Newsletter*. Yorkshire, Eng.: Squadron Association Committee, 1992–2002.

Tomkins, M. "A Memory of the Cold War." *Air Mail*, July/Sept. 1999.

PHOTO BY HEATHER MacDONALD

About the Author

Joan Hemingway MacDonald was born in Wakefield, Yorkshire, England, in 1922. She was a member of a British political family. Her father and brother were both involved in local politics; her father was mayor of the City of Wakefield in 1936.

During World War Two, at the age of nineteen, she joined the Women's Auxiliary Air Force (WAAF) for "the duration of emergency." For most of her time in the air force she was stationed at Holme on Spalding Moor bomber base, where she was the non-commissioned officer in charge of the Teleprinter Section.

She married Flight Lieutenant Malcolm MacDonald, DFC, a Halifax bomber pilot who flew operations from Holme on Spalding Moor. She came to Canada as a war bride in 1946.

Mrs. MacDonald is a freelance writer who has been published in *Canadian Legion*, *World War Two*, *The Rotarian*, *Western People*, *Living History*, etc., and has had several children's stories published. She was the development officer at Stanstead College and her book, *The Stanstead College Story*, was published in 1977.

The MacDonalds live in Stanstead, Quebec. They have three children and two grandchildren.